THE HONORABLE POWELL CLAYTON

The
Honorable
Powell
Clayton

William H. Burnside

UCA Press
1991

© 1991 by UCA Press

ISBN 0-944436-10-2

To Jeannine

Acknowledgments

This biography grew from my doctoral dissertation on Powell Clayton's diplomatic career. For both works I am indebted to Dr. Willard B. Gatewood, Jr., Distinguished Professor of History at the University of Arkansas, for ideas, encouragement, and valuable criticism. Similar encouragement and ideas came from my colleague and friend at John Brown University, Dr. Richard Niswonger. Thanks also are due my professional critics, whose observations, though caustic, have been invaluable in improving this work. Warmer thanks must be acknowledged for the kind, patient and persistent help from the capable editor of UCA Press, Bob Lowrey. His encouragement and insights helped bring this project to fruition.

Initial impetus for this biography came from an unexpected source. Howard Westwood, an attorney in Washington, D.C., read my dissertation several years ago and brought it to the attention of Powell Clayton's great grandson, Vincent Goffinet, who then invited us to Belgium. There we met Clayton's granddaughter, Kathleen, and learned more details of family history. I am indebted to Vincent and his wife Joelle and Kathleen's daughter, Diane Medlicott, who together with her husband Ronald, entrusted to us family letters pertaining to Powell Clayton. We visited the Medlicotts twice in England and value their hospitality and friendship.

I would be remiss if I failed to acknowledge the encouragement of my four children: Jeannine, Bill, Cheryl, and Jon. They have watched with interest the creative process of publishing this book and have given me nine grandchildren during the time I spent writing it. Michelle, Wendy, Nicole, Colin, Julie, Rachelle, Amy, Rory, and Annabel are a bit bewildered, but excited that Papaw's book is finally being published.

As with all my work, my wife Minnie has been an ever-present encouragement to her husband. The summer we spent in New Hampshire revising the manuscript and visiting Clayton's favorite vacation spots on the coast of Maine, is remembered fondly. So is our visit to Belgium and England with time out to celebrate our 25th anniversary in Switzerland.

This book is dedicated to my oldest daughter, Mrs. Jeannine Little, because she, more than anyone else, had a direct role in research, writing, and criticism of the manuscript. When she was an eighth grade student, she helped her father read microfilm, searching for preliminary material on his dissertation and eventually typed the entire manuscript. Later as a mature career woman and mother, she offered perceptive advice and gentle criticism. Her help was invaluable, but her cheerful companionship was worth even more.

CONTENTS

Dedication   v

Acknowledgements   vi

Prologue   1

Chapter I: General Clayton   3

Chapter II: Governor Clayton   25

Chapter III: Senator Clayton   51

Chapter IV: Mister Clayton   63

Chapter V: Boss Clayton   73

Chapter VI: Ambassador Clayton   93

Chapter VII: Powell Clayton   115

Epilogue   127

Sources   129

PROLOGUE

Americans take pride in their constitutional prohibition banning titles of nobility. Seeking a more democratic society, they have acquired class mobility. There is a certain anomaly in this, however. Achievement-oriented nineteenth-century Americans often used official titles to help perpetuate their status. Powell Clayton, for example, served briefly as Brigadier General in the Union Army at the age of thirty-one and was Governor of Arkansas for only three years. Fifty years later, however, he was often still called "General" or "Governor Clayton."

Clayton was most famous as Governor of Arkansas during Reconstruction. He was also successful in several other careers and his titles reflected that success. Six years as United States Senator followed his governorship. Those two political experiences launched him into life-long participation in Republican national politics. As boss of the Arkansas Republican state organization, he exerted considerable influence at both the state and national levels. His prestige and administrative abilities enabled him to pursue a concurrent business career, particularly in the building of the picturesque resort town of Eureka Springs, Arkansas. Clayton's political contributions were rewarded with an ambassadorship to Mexico, a prestigious post from which Clayton continued to dominate Arkansas Republican politics.

This is the story of one American politician's life. It is not the account of a charismatic political leader attracting votes but rather of a professional politician influencing other professionals. Clayton was a persistent and dependable party chieftain, the kind of man who made Gilded Age Republican politics work so successfully.

Chapter One

GENERAL CLAYTON

Powell Clayton's Quaker ancestors came to America with William Penn in the late seventeenth century. His mother was the daughter of a British army officer and his father, an orchard-keeper and carpenter, was active in Whig politics. Born on 7 August 1833 in Bethel County, Pennsylvania, Powell spent his early years on the family farm with his three brothers. He attended Partridge Military Academy at Bristol, Pennsylvania, and then studied civil engineering in Wilmington, Delaware.

Seeking a place to use his new surveying skills, Clayton, at age twenty-two, moved to Leavenworth, Kansas, in 1855. Kansas Territory had just been opened to non-Indian settlement the year before and hundreds of towns immediately sprang up, especially near the Missouri River. Promoters and investors saw town building as a quick road to riches, especially on railroad routes and navigable rivers that connected with the Missouri. In 1857 Clayton and four other men incorporated a new little town on the Big Blue River north of Leavenworth. The town did not prosper, however, and became one of the hundreds of "lost" towns of Kansas.

Leavenworth was one of the first and largest towns built in the new territory. Located on the Missouri River with a good harbor for steamboat traffic, Leavenworth became a supply town for northeastern Kansas, for overland travel, and for the Colorado mines near Pikes Peak. By 1859 it had a population of 11,000 plus hundreds of transients. The six years Powell Clayton lived in Leavenworth brought him experiences and insights into living in a turbulent political environment. He participated in the building of a frontier town and experienced the dynamism and dangers of a new and energetic society. Later in life Clayton drew on his Leavenworth experiences in his war with guerrillas in Arkansas; in coping with a hostile and violent political opposition when he was governor of Arkansas; and still later, in building the resort town of Eureka Springs, Arkansas. Leavenworth provided a model in Clayton's mind of what a civilized town in a primitive area should look like.

During the time Clayton lived in Leavenworth, the town had four daily newspapers including one German language paper. The diverse ethnic population included large numbers of single young men like Powell

Clayton seeking their fortune in the new land. A "Merry Bachelors' Ball" on Valentine's Day, 1859, was attended also by "maids and matrons, mothers and daughters, and widows." The dirt streets were lined with dry goods emporiums, bakeries, grocery markets, print shops, book stores, furniture establishments, leather shops, lumber yards, blacksmiths and chimney specialists, and fruit and confectionery shops. Many boarding houses and hotels competed for clients, and Beebe's Bowling Saloon always advertised a free lunch. "Swede Cloth Dress" and "Ottoman Velvet" were available, and for gentlemen, "a rich and beautiful assortment of French Broad Cloth for Coats and Overcoats, Fancy and Plain French Cashmeres for pantaloons, and Plain and Fancy Velvets and Silks for Vests."

To enhance the culture of the new town "local talent" and visiting musicians on a travel circuit performed regular evening concerts. In 1859 the Leavenworth *Times* thought that "the girls of Miss Perrin's school looked beautiful and sang charmingly." The *Times* reporter was especially pleased with "Rocked in the Cradle of the Deep." The National Theatre often filled to see famous actors or a "celebrated tragedienne." *Still Waters Run Deep* was a popular comedy as was *Faint Heart*. *Othello* was not well-attended that year because the weather was "nasty, gloomy, disagreeable, windy, snowy, misty, rainy, sleety, and dirty."[1]

Clayton had the opportunity to attend a variety of churches: Methodist, Episcopal, Congregational, Christian, Catholic, Baptist, and three Presbyterian congregations. The Leavenworth Bible Society met annually and distributed free Bibles and testaments to the entire city three times between 1856 and 1861. In 1859 the voters of Leavenworth by a vote of 1,027 to 621 approved a "Sunday law" which mandated Sunday closings of businesses in the city. By 1861 Leavenworth had five public schools: primary, intermediate, and a grammar school, employing five teachers for 261 pupils. Leavenworth College opened in 1859.

Leavenworth had two hundred licensed saloons. A local minister described that side of life in December, 1862:

> We have two theatres of a low order much patronized. Saloons and whiskey shops almost numberless; about 300 prostitutes; whose houses are very prominent and notorious, one of which stands right in front of the Methodist Church, unmolested by Civil authority. A very large proportion of our citizens are young men, away from home and also without the restraints of well-organized and virtuous society and they fall ready victims of the temptations that assail them on all hands. Many of them are intelligent and, have been well-educated under early religious influences, and are respectable as the world goes. . . .[2]

The newspapers of the town regularly warned "Emigrants" to be on their guard for "sharpers and swindlers" and pickpockets who "infest the boats, the cities, and even the plains." There were even "female highway-men" who robbed farmers returning from market. Murders were often reported and accidental drownings in the Missouri were common. Fires were a perennial problem and entire blocks burned at times despite vig-orous efforts by volunteer fire companies. Pigs and stray animals wandered the often-muddy streets, scavenging. Public meetings were held to discuss philosophic issues such as "Is man a free moral agent?" The YMCA or-ganized such meetings and Gentlemen and Ladies were both invited. A city Relief Committee regularly aided the transient destitute.

Clayton began surveying work and was eventually elected City En-gineer, a position which included surveying for streets, building bridges and heavy plank sidewalks, and erecting lamp posts. He was also on the Committee of Arrangements to help organize a "Great Celebration" to welcome the return of the first line of express coaches from Pikes Peak in 1859. Clayton lived in the Mansion House, a large hotel that was a gath-ering-place for immigrants from the Free States.[3]

Kansas was in turmoil as the nation focused on the issue of slavery in the territories. The Kansas-Nebraska Act of 1854 introduced the concept of "popular sovereignty" to the slavery issue in Kansas and both north and south sought to encourage either free-state or proslavery immigrants into Kansas. Proslavery men controlled the city government of Leavenworth in 1855 and had their own vigilance committee of fifty to prevent free-state men from voting. In the summer of 1856 seventy-five Illinois settlers were robbed of their equipment and tools and forced to go down river on the *Star of the West*. In September 1856 a proslavery band of eight hundred sought to drive out of Leavenworth all free state settlers. One hundred men, women, and children were driven aboard the steamboat *Emma* and fifty more sent down-river on the *Polar Star*.

The territorial governor John Geary took vigorous action and ordered the disbanding of the militia and enforced his order with federal troops from nearby Fort Leavenworth. When a free election was held in 1857 without intimidation, a free state mayor and city council were elected and free state settlers continued to pour into the city. Republicans controlled all seven city offices and most of the city council in 1860 and 1861 when Clayton was elected City Engineer.[4]

On 21 May 1856 Missourians invaded Lawrence, Kansas, a center for free state settlers some thirty miles from Leavenworth. The border ruffians burned the Free-State Hotel, wrecked two newspaper offices after dumping their printing presses into the river, killed several people, and

Kansas and the Civil War on the Border

looted homes and stores. Fifty or so free state men called the Pottawato-
mie Rifles went to the relief of Lawrence, but not until the invaders had
returned to Missouri. Most of the Kansans returned home, but John Brown,
Sr., and seven others decided a little revenge was in order. They found
several isolated proslavery cabins and shot or hacked to death five men
who had no connection with the sack of Lawrence. These events turned
the Kansas-Missouri border into a battlefield and Kansas Territory became
"Bleeding Kansas." Hangings, lootings, burnings, and armed warfare became commonplace. In 1856 alone two hundred lives were taken violently.

Free soilers developed a network of informers to learn the names and
places of residence of border ruffians and sought to burn them out in Missouri. Their intelligence system sometimes enabled them to intercept a
raiding party and pre-empt an attack. At times the United States government tried to restore order. United States marshals called for military
assistance and soldiers from Fort Scott and Fort Leavenworth sought to

capture border ruffians and jayhawkers alike. (The hawk symbolized the Kansans pouncing on the robber jays.) In 1860 General William Harney went in force to Fort Scott and sent two companies of infantry to Mound City under the command of Captain Nathaniel Lyon, soon to become famous for his preservation of St. Louis and Missouri for the Union.[5]

As far as the available evidence shows, Powell Clayton was not directly involved in these events except to help provide for the defense of the city of Leavenworth. However, the type of vicious warfare that he saw in Kansas and Missouri, together with the continuing political struggle in Kansas helped to prepare him for the guerrilla warfare he would contend with in Arkansas during the Civil War, and the political struggle helped to prepare him for his position of Reconstruction Governor of Arkansas.

Political violence between Democrats and Republicans was not unusual. On the night of 3 September 1859 a torch-light street brawl occurred between the rival parties. The (Republican) Leavenworth *Times* explained that Delaware and Second was Republican territory and when Democrats marched in a torch-light procession past that corner, "of course they were stopped and difficulty occurred." By the look of the many torches scattered along Second Street and up Main, it must have been quite a melee. The *Times* commended Judge John A. Halderman for trying to defuse the situation and considered him "among the sturdiest of our political opponents."

As war approached, many pro-Union Democrats clashed with their pro-Confederate fellow Democrats and

Colonel Powell Clayton

Democratic meetings were often quite heated. When the war finally began, Democrats as well as Republicans enlisted on the Union side. John Halderman was appointed a major in the First Kansas Infantry and Captain Powell Clayton was one of the regiment's company commanders. They became close personal friends and kept in contact later in life. Halderman was later elected mayor of Leavenworth.

The four hundred young Republicans who belonged to the "Wide Awake Club" met at Mozart Hall in August, 1860, in an effort to reform city government. The Tuesday election the next week brought to administrative office nine Republicans who also won five out of eight council seats. The Independent Democratic ticket in that election reflected the North-South split in the Democratic Party.

Republicans, too, were split over secession. The Leavenworth *Times* wrote editorially on 16 November 1860: "Dear as this Union is to every true patriot, it cannot be maintained in its original spirit, if allegiance to it must be secured by force of arms." Nevertheless, when war did come, Kansans, both Republican and Democrat, flocked to the Union colors. The (Democratic) Leavenworth *Herald* made its stand clear on 3 April 1861: The *Herald*, it wrote, "will hereafter advocate the maintenance of the Union."[6]

Kansas was admitted to the Union on 29 January 1861 and elected Republican Charles Robinson as its first governor. Political patronage thus shifted from Democratic to Republican control, particularly after the inauguration of Republican President Abraham Lincoln on 4 March 1861. The new governor had the authority to appoint and commission all field and staff officers of Kansas regiments. This authority, however, was challenged by the Republican political rival of the governor, United States Senator James Lane who sought authority directly from the War Department to appoint regiments of his own.

Governor Robinson on 28 May 1861 appointed Colonel George Deitzler of

Battle of Wilson's Creek Campaign Area

Lawrence to organize the First Kansas Infantry. Deitzler had been Speaker of the House in the 1858 territorial legislature. He appointed to his staff Major John Halderman of Leavenworth. It was customary for soldiers to choose their own company commanders, and Leavenworth had already formed a dozen militia companies: Union Guard, German Citizen Guard, Leavenworth Light Infantry, Leavenworth City Guards, Leavenworth Rifles, Mounted Rifle Company, and others. The Leavenworth Light Infantry elected Powell Clayton as captain and became Company E of the First Kansas Infantry.[7]

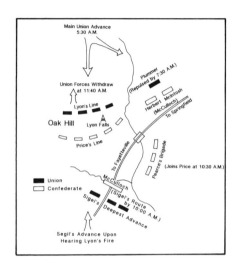

Battle of Wilson's Creek

Young, aggressive, and efficient, Clayton was a capable officer. His army photograph reveals alert, dark eyes and a tight-lipped, determined appearance. His weather-beaten face, receding hairline, and unkempt mustache and goatee made him appear older than his twenty-seven years. Of medium height and a "graceful, haughty bearing," Clayton was well-known for his personal courage, suave demeanor, and fiery temper. Confederate General John Marmaduke, the cavalry commander who opposed him at Pine Bluff, considered Clayton "the ablest federal commander of cavalry west of the Mississippi."

During the early months of 1861, Kansas carefully watched developments in Missouri and prepared for war. If Missouri seceded from the Union, Kansas would be largely isolated and would be in danger of attack from Missouri. There was also a militant proslavery minority in Kansas which already had led to guerrilla warfare among neighbors.

Events in Missouri were so crucial to Kansas that when pro-Confederate Missouri Governor Claiborne Jackson called for 50,000 troops to resist an "invasion" from the United States, Governor Robinson sent three regiments, including the First Kansas Infantry, to reinforce General Nathaniel Lyon in Missouri. General Lyon appointed Major Halderman Provost Marshal General of his army.

Confederate troops in Arkansas reinforced Missouri forces at Wilson's

Creek, twelve miles southwest of Springfield, outnumbering federal troops more than two to one. On 10 August 1861 General Lyon sought to take control of Oak Hill, the high ground overlooking the enemy position along Wilson's Creek. He divided his forces into two divisions, planning a simultaneous front and rear assault. Lyon's main force occupied Oak Hill, and began firing on the Confederate position below. For six hours one Confederate assault after another sought to dislodge Union troops. The First Kansas was in the hardest fighting on Oak Hill. Captain Clayton's Company E lost 49 men, more than any other unit in the battle.

When the Union position finally could no longer be held, the regimental commander ordered a retreat, but in the midst of the noise, confusion, and smoke of battle, Clayton did not hear the order and advanced while the other companies in his regiment withdrew. His decimated company topped a rise and saw a group of men clad in blue-gray uniforms who appeared to be Union troops. Clayton suddenly recognized the commanding officer as the former postmaster at Leavenworth, whom he knew to be Confederate. Immediately Clayton's men began edging away while the adjutant of the Confederate force galloped towards them and commanded them to halt.

Clayton shouted an about face and his men faced the enemy with rifles ready. The confederate adjutant called to Clayton, "What troops are these?" Ignoring the question, Clayton shouted to him, "Confederate or United States?" "Confederate!" replied the mounted officer. "Then dismount,—damn you! You're my prisoner," bellowed Clayton, drawing his pistol. The adjutant obeyed. "Now order your men not to fire or you're a dead man," said Clayton, moving backwards with his men, keeping the Confederate officer between the two groups of soldiers.

Suddenly Clayton's prisoner, with incredible bravery, ordered his men to fire on the Union soldiers. Instantly Clayton shot him and a sergeant thrust his bayonet through the officer's body, pinning him to the ground. The Union troops ran for their lives, re-grouped on the other side of the hill and escaped. Clayton's company was cited for gallantry in action. General Lyon was killed at Wilson's Creek, and losses were heavy on both sides in this first major battle in the West. Union troops withdrew to Rolla, but Confederates did not press their advantage.[8]

After the battle of Wilson's Creek, Clayton was promoted to Lieutenant Colonel and given command of the Fifth Kansas Cavalry on 1 February 1862. Clayton's rapid promotion was due to his bravery and coolness under fire and was not a political appointment. The Fifth Kansas Cavalry began as part of "Lane's Brigade," a nickname for the regiments recruited by Senator James Lane. After the battle of Wilson's Creek the Senator himself led his troops back into Kansas in an effort to protect the new state from an anticipated Confederate invasion under General Sterling Price, former Governor of Missouri. As he crossed Missouri, Lane destroyed pro-Confederate towns en route. In one of these raids the regimental commander of the Fifth Kansas, Colonel Hampton Johnson, was killed leading a wild charge through the streets of Morristown, Missouri. Senator Lane replaced him with an exceptionally unpopular officer, Lieutenant Colonel John Ritchy. At a "tumultuous mass meeting" at Osawatomie and at Fort Lincoln, the men of his regiment demanded his replacement. Their demand was heeded and Powell Clayton was promoted to regimental commander about the same time that a new Department of Kansas was created by the War Department under the command of General David Hunter. Senator Lane returned to Washington and the First Kansas returned in triumph to Leavenworth for a victory parade and celebration of Colonel Deitzler's promotion to Brigadier General.

The *Daily Times* called attention to the "honorable distinction" Lieutenant Colonel Powell Clayton had won in the army and commented that Clayton was "of the stuff that soldiers are made of *sans peur et sans reproche* and will lead the Kansas Boys to victory or to death with equal courage and daring. Powell is one of the bravest, most energetic and dashing officers in the service."[9]

According to one of the company commanders of the Fifth Kansas Cavalry, Colonel Clayton "by discreet management speedily created order out of chaos" constantly drilling his men in cavalry exercises. Morale and discipline quickly improved under Clayton and the Fifth Kansas was soon ordered from Fort Scott, Kansas, back into Missouri. While other Union troops pushed into Northwest Arkansas and confronted Confederate forces during three days of heavy fighting near Pea Ridge, Powell Clayton and his Kansas cavalry sought to secure a firmer Union control of Missouri. Rebel guerrilla raids were an ever-present danger in Union-held territory where a large percentage of civilians were sympathetic to the South. Home Guards were organized for local defense and regular Union troops such as the Fifth Kansas patrolled insofar as they were able.

Clayton's troops captured Carthage on 16 March 1862 and soon moved on to Springfield. About twenty miles away in the village of Rock Prairie, Union men and property had been destroyed by guerrillas. The Fifth Kansas retaliated by burning twenty houses and killing or hanging a dozen guerrillas without any Union losses. The cavalry escorted supply trains and paymasters and made several incursions into the countryside as a show of strength. Confederate irregulars let them pass and continued their activities unmolested. Clayton pushed on to Rolla and then to Batesville, Arkansas, making several expeditions up and down the White River, fighting regular skirmishes with guerrillas before reaching his destination of Helena.[10]

The Civil War in Arkansas was a combination of guerrilla warfare and traditional strategic maneuvering. Clayton's Fifth Kansas was part of the Union army which occupied Helena, Arkansas, an important supply depot on the Mississippi River. This was part of the key Union objective of gaining control of the entire length of the Mississippi River. At the same time cavalry units such as Clayton's often penetrated the countryside with regular patrols. Much of Arkansas was in a state of anarchy, dominated by various bands of armed men. Some were Unionist in sympathy and others were pro-Confederacy. Many others were simply outlaws, robbers, and bushwhackers who sought to prey on the unfortunate settlers and travelers who passed by. The result was a mass exodus from Arkansas whenever a wagon train could find enough armed men to escort it to safer areas. Union sympathizers fled to central Missouri and pro-Southerners sought refuge in south Arkansas and in Texas.[11]

The Union government in Washington and the Confederate government in Richmond both recognized the predominant importance of the eastern theatres of war compared to the trans-Mississippi and consequently concentrated their troops in the East. Arkansas Governor Henry Rector, angered over what he considered the abandonment of Arkansas by the Confederate government, issued a call for state troops to defend Arkansas and hinted that it might become necessary for the state to secede from the Confederate States of America if Arkansas had to provide for its own defense. In response Major General Earl Van Dorn appointed General Thomas C. Hindman to organize Confederate defenses in Arkansas. By persuasion and threats of conscription and martial law, Hindman succeeded in raising a substantial Confederate force in Arkansas.[12]

Meanwhile on 25 November 1862 the Fifth Kansas Cavalry crossed the Mississippi River as part of a Union army of 10,000 infantry and 1,800 cavalry on a search and destroy mission to Grenada, Mississippi. This also protected any movement in force against General William Sherman's unsuccessful assault on Chickasaw Bluffs in his attempt to approach Vicksburg from the North. After some success in destroying railroads and railroad bridges, the army returned to Helena, seeking to expand Union control of the eastern Arkansas river, preparatory to an anticipated assault on Little Rock.

In January, 1863, General John McClernand with 32,000 troops, 3 ironclads, and 6 gunboats, captured Arkansas Post, southwest of Helena, while Colonel Clayton simultaneously sought to capture St. Charles. High water forced Clayton to move against Clarendon instead. When his men captured two rebel pickets, they learned of an intended rendezvous of Confederate soldiers with some Arkansas girls in La Grange. Late that night Clayton's men surrounded the rendezvous house, killed one fleeing soldier, wounded several others, and took six prisoners without any Union casualties.

On 5-12 March 1863 Clayton took part of his regiment up the Saint Francis River to the village of Madison, Arkansas, where the Memphis and Little Rock Railroad crossed the river. Aboard the steamer *Hamilton Belle*, his troops arrived at the unsuspecting town shortly after daylight.

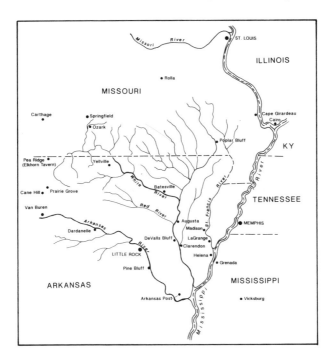

Missouri-Arkansas Borderland

The steamer, concealed from view until it was within a few hundred yards of Madison, completely surprised a group of seventy-five Confederate soldiers who fled in confusion as the Union cavalry and infantry pursued them and captured twenty-seven men, arms, horses, and equipment. Clayton's little band of eighty-five men ventured many miles from Helena before beginning the return journey, which Clayton expected to be impeded by Confederate guerrillas. Using sixty-four bales of confiscated cotton, the Colonel constructed defenses along the deck of his ship. Carefully approaching the town of Madison again, Clayton noticed several bales of cotton on the bank. Suspecting a trap, he shelled the area and swept the underbrush with canister shot. Spotting a large number of saddled horses, he immediately landed his entire force and, leaving about half of them as a reserve to protect the ship and a possible retreat, pursued the enemy in a running fight. When the guerrillas fled, four of their number lay dead. Clayton's men suffered one casualty.

Back aboard the *Hamilton Belle*, the Fifth Kansas discovered that a great chain had been drawn between piers of a railroad bridge, obstructing passage. Clayton sent a working party under armed protection to remove the blockade. A brief skirmish ensued and once past the obstacle, Clayton's ship received a heavy volley from a canebrake on the right bank. Twenty-five rounds from his artillery guns took care of the problem and harassment ceased for the remainder of the return trip. The Fifth Kansas had captured forty-six prisoners, some food and cotton, and twenty-six horses and mules. The hardships had been many, of course, including contending with the "contemptible little fly called Buffalo gnat" which killed at least one hundred of their horses.

On 6 May 1863 Colonel Clayton was given 800 infantry and 1000 cavalry for an expedition to destroy all forage, provisions, and mills between the Mississippi River and the White River. In one skirmish the Union cavalry discovered that their opponents were armed only with shotguns and drove them back easily with their longer-range Sharp's

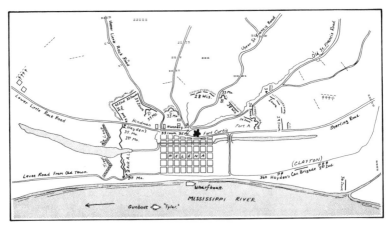

Union Field Works around Helena

carbines. Clayton was attacked by a force of 1600 Texas Rangers, but held his ground with few losses. The Union soldiers destroyed a steam mill and 75,000 bushels of corn and returned to Helena.

One would think that Clayton would be ready by then for a bit of rest and relaxation. Perhaps so, but his recreation took the form of a "sham" battle between Union cavalry and artillery on 22 May 1863, inspired, according to one of his company commanders, by "the intoxicating bowl." Clayton and the commander of an artillery battery argued over the number of times the artillery could fire before the Fifth Kansas could sweep across two hundred yards and overwhelm it in a cavalry charge. Despite

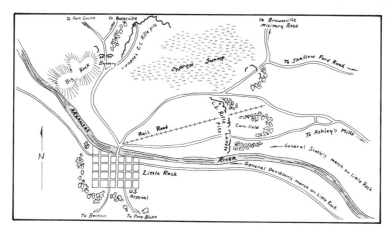

Little Rock and the Rebel Field-Works

protestations by nearly all the regimental officers, six artillery guns were loaded with blank cartridges and the Kansas cavalry charged and vanquished the artillery. However, in the dense clouds of smoke fifteen men were thrown from their horses and several were severely injured.[13]

Union troops used Helena as an important supply depot for the Vicksburg campaign. To relieve pressure on Vicksburg, the confederate military command massed 8,000 troops for an assault on Helena, ironically for 4 July 1863, the date Vicksburg fell to Union forces. The 4,100 troops defending Helena had strong fortifications on the steep hills overlooking the town. The gunboat *Tyler* with its 8-inch guns gave additional support. Clayton, with dismounted troops of the Fifth Kansas and the First Indiana, defended a levee north of Helena and held the right flank of the Union lines for seven hours, losing twenty-four men in the attack. The Confederates captured Graveyard Hill overlooking both Helena and Fort Curtis, but Clayton's brigade tenaciously prevented a Confederate advance towards Fort Curtis on Sterling Road. Guns from Fort Curtis and three artillery batteries subjected Graveyard Hill to a fierce bombardment supported by the gunboat in the Mississippi River. The Confederates withdrew after several hours with 1,636 losses compared to 239 Union casualties.

The Union Commander at Helena, Major General Benjamin Prentiss thought the Confederates were regrouping for a renewed assault since they had a numerical superiority. When the expected attack failed to materialize after two days, Prentiss sent a strong cavalry patrol commanded by Clayton to reconnoiter. The patrol failed to observe a yellow hospital flag on a farm near Helena and opened fire, but no one was hurt.[14]

Failure to wrest Helena from Union control prompted a Confederate withdrawal to Little Rock and continued Union occupation of Arkansas Post, Clarendon, Devall's Bluff, and Helena. Early in August 1863 the Arkansas Expedition Army, with approximately 13,000 men, left Helena under the command of Major General Frederick Steele. Nearly half of those troops consisted of Brigadier General John W. Davidson's cavalry division. Powell Clayton commanded one of Davidson's brigades, which included the Fifth Kansas Cavalry, the First Indiana, and the Tenth and Thirteenth Illinois. The cavalry was in the advance and saw action at several locations en route to Little Rock. Between the White River and Bayou Meto, Davidson's cavalry skirmished almost daily with Confederate General John Marmaduke's rear guard. Numerically superior federal troops forced the Confederates to withdraw from every position they held en route.

Strategically located on the Arkansas River, Little Rock was the capital and largest city in Arkansas with a population of 3,700. It was a difficult city to defend since the river was fordable in a dozen places. Fortifications north of the river were obviously ineffective if Davidson and Clayton attacked the town from the south, which they did, forcing the strategic withdrawal of Confederate troops north of the river. On 10 September 1863 Commanding General Sterling Price ordered his Confederate troops to retreat south towards Arkadelphia. Colonel Clayton's brigade pursued them 20 miles, skirmished with the rear guard, and captured 250 prisoners. A few months later, Fort Smith fell to federal troops and Arkansas appeared to be divided into Union territory north of the Arkansas River and confederate territory south. In reality guerrilla warfare continued on both sides of the river. Large troop concentrations of both Union and Confederate operated with little regard for a supposed strategic line.

After the fall of Little Rock, General Steele sent Colonel Clayton to occupy Pine Bluff and pacify the surrounding countryside. Pine Bluff, fifty miles southeast of Little Rock, was a key stronghold on the Arkansas River. Clayton assumed command early in October 1863 and moved 300 troops and 4 mountain howitzers into Confederate-held territory. On 11 October 1863 his cavalry routed 200 Confederates in a surprise dawn attack at the village of Tulip, 35 miles from Pine Bluff, and returned with captured supplies and wagons. Slightly wounded by a glancing shot, Colonel Clayton was the only Union casualty.[15]

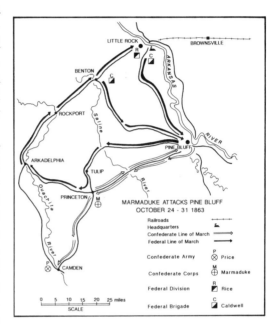

MARMADUKE ATTACKS PINE BLUFF
OCTOBER 24 - 31 1863

The Civil War in Arkansas resumed its typical characteristic as guerrilla warfare until 24 October 1863 when Confederate General John Marmaduke approached Pine Bluff with a force of 2,000 and 12 artillery guns. With a superior number of men, Marmaduke intended to attack simultaneously from the west and from the south. The Union army, backed up to the Arkansas River, could be caught in a squeeze and annihilated or forced to flee across the river.

Meanwhile Clayton organized the defense of the city. He fortified the streets leading into the courthouse square with cotton bales and light artillery and posted sharpshooters in the buildings facing the square. Union troops numbered fewer than six hundred.

Early in the morning of 25 October 1863, a young lieutenant on a reconnaissance patrol skirmished with the advance elements of General Marmaduke's command. Under a flag of truce the Confederate officer asked for a surrender of Pine Bluff. The Lieutenant replied,

> Colonel Clayton never surrenders, but is always anxious for you to come and take him, and you must get back to your command immediately, or I will order my men to fire on you.

For seven hours enemy artillery and infantry forced the Union de-
fenders back towards the town square and courthouse and drove them out
of several buildings, which the attackers burned, including the living
quarters of the Fifth Kansas Cavalry.

General Marmaduke deployed his troops to cut off all lines of escape,
but there seemed to be no thought of escape in Clayton's mind. He knew
he had a strong position and he intended to hold it. Three Confederate
batteries engaged Union artillery in a fierce duel. Wherever Confederate
infantry probed, they met scathing fire. By the middle of the afternoon,
Marmaduke decided to abandon the attack. He calculated that a frontal
assault against the Union barricades would cost at least five hundred casualties, a loss he was unwilling to sustain. Colonel Clayton's command had
succeeded in repelling an assault by a superior force and retained control
of Pine Bluff and an important section of the Arkansas River. It was a
spectacular victory and congratulatory messages came from many sources.
Not only was the defense heroic but Clayton commended 200 newly-freed
blacks who put up barricades and put out fires for bravery under fire.
Confederate casualties numbered 41, about the same as Union losses. Marmaduke wrote in his report, "My troops behaved well. The federals fought
like devils."[16]

When reinforcements from General Steele arrived in Pine Bluff,
Clayton ordered them to pursue Marmaduke, who was at Princeton, forty
miles southwest. Marmaduke moved south to Camden and Clayton's
troops captured Arkadelphia and turned north to Benton. En route they
captured many horses and mules, several prisoners, and Confederate mail
including $1,370.

In the spring of 1864 the next phase of the grand strategy of the
Union was put into motion: split the South by cutting Louisiana in half
and marching across Texas to the Gulf of Mexico. The task was entrusted
to former speaker of the House Major General Nathaniel Banks and came
to be known as the Red River expedition. Banks captured Alexandria,
Louisiana, and began pushing north up the Red river towards Shreveport.
His army of 17,000 was to be reinforced with 10,000 from Tennessee and
General Frederick Steele was to join him from Little Rock with 15,000
soldiers. Steele attacked Camden and ordered Clayton to leave a garrison
at Pine Bluff and move towards Monticello, hoping that his own troops
would be able to drive Confederate forces from Camden into Clayton's
waiting guns. At Mount Elba Clayton himself, hat in hand, led a cavalry
charge on a Confederate position. According to Clayton's official report,
"the enemy broke in the wildest confusion. . . . The road and timber were

strewn with blankets, saddlebags, hats, and guns. . . ."

Clayton's troops followed up their advantage, but not before retreating Confederate soldiers destroyed a bridge over a swollen creek which could not be forded. Clayton decided to return to Pine Bluff with the prisoners and contraband his men had captured: 300 prisoners, 300 horses and mules, and $60,000 from a paymaster's safe.

A few days later, however, two of General Steele's brigades met with disaster at Poison Spring and at Marks' Mills. Food supplies had run low in Camden so Steele sent a forage train of 200 wagons to confiscate 5,000 bushels of corn known to be at Poison Spring. The escort numbered 1,160 men. On 18 April 1864 they were attacked by 3,335 Confederate cavalry and mounted infantry. Union casualties numbered 301, including wounded soldiers killed without mercy. The First Kansas Colored Volunteers lost 117 killed and 65 wounded out of 438 in the regiment. The Union commander wrote: "I have the most positive assurance from eyewitnesses that [black prisoners] were murdered on the spot." The Confederate Second Indian Brigade scalped those they killed. Confederate casualties totaled 114. Just two days later Colonel Clayton's supply train from Pine Bluff reached Camden. On its return trip Confederates captured all 240 wagons and took 1,300 prisoners at Marks' Mills.[17]

General Steele, by then outnumbered at Camden and surrounded

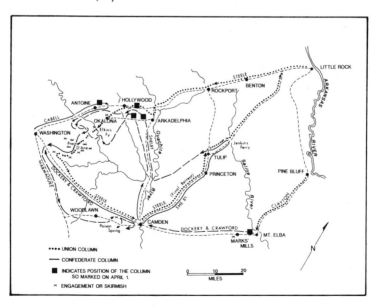

Union and Confederate lines of march during the Camden Expedition,
March 23 to May 3, 1864

by Confederate troops, built a pontoon bridge across the Ouachita River and fought his way north towards Little Rock with heavy losses. The last major battle of the Red River/Camden Expedition was fought 30 April 1864 at Jenkins' Ferry, thirty-five miles south of Little Rock. That fierce battle resulted in 521 Union casualties and 443 Confederate. General Steele continued his retreat to Little Rock and word reached him that the Red River campaign had failed. The Union would concentrate on taking Atlanta and then cut through Georgia to the sea. Union troops in Arkansas would try to hold what they had.

Both Steele and Clayton knew that the Confederates had great

strength in southern Arkansas, and Pine Bluff could well be a prime target. If Confederate objectives had included Pine Bluff, it was unlikely that Clayton's relatively small garrison could have withstood a determined attack in strength. Such an assault, however, was not the purpose of Confederate troop concentrations. Late in August 1864 General Sterling Price with 12,000 mounted men made an extraordinarily reckless cavalry raid into Missouri and Kansas. At Westport, Missouri, he was blocked for a time by 20,000 federal troops. Price's sweep of some fifteen hundred miles was a desperate effort by the western Confederacy to "do some-

Courthouse at Pine Bluff

thing." The raid inflicted considerable property damage but relatively few casualties and, strategically, was worthless. Price's "*ad hoc* army melted away" during the long retreat through Missouri and Arkansas towards Texas.[18]

In October, Clayton again reported a concentration of Confederate infantry near Pine Bluff and at Monticello. Steele sent him 777 Cavalry and Clayton added 250 of his own for a reconnaissance patrol. A sharp engagement occurred at Hurricane Creek but was of little consequence. Only minor skirmishes took place from then until the end of the war.

A few months before the war ended, President Abraham Lincoln promoted Colonel Clayton to Brigadier General. Steele wrote to the new general on 26 August 1864 that he and his staff and "everybody in this city whose good opinion is worth having" were "in ecstasy" over his promotion. On 13 May 1865 General Clayton was given command of the Cavalry Brigade, Seventh Army Corps, Little Rock.[19]

Clayton was an able military commander. He demonstrated courage, stability, and decisiveness. His superior officers respected him and so did his men. Obviously his experiences as a wartime commander left a permanent impression on Clayton's personality, philosophy, and political career. The Confederate massacre of black prisoners at Poison Spring, Fort Pillow (north of Memphis) and elsewhere pointed toward the kind of political terrorism that occurred during Reconstruction. Indeed, brutal slaughter of opponents was often characteristic of the Civil War in Kansas, Missouri, and Arkansas. Dealing with those atrocities and guerrilla warfare in general were part of Clayton's military experiences that helped to prepare him for his role as Reconstruction Governor of Arkansas.

Clayton's military experience accustomed him to the hierarchical structure of the army and he often saw political structure in much the same way. He saw the importance of a forceful recommendation from one's immediate superior officer in securing promotions. He realized that subordinates simply must perform effectively if the commander is to fulfill his responsibilities. For those who did, the commanding officer wrote favorable reports. For those who did not, the opposite was done. Later in politics he often said that "those who do the work should receive the rewards." Clayton was a tough "boss" but he was also a loyal party man. He "closed ranks" behind the party nominee and worked for the benefit of the regular party establishment. Clayton was not interested in political *coups d'état* or disruptive intrigues within his own party.

Powell Clayton's army career gave him extensive experience in positions of great responsibility. He eagerly accepted the duties of his position and expected to have concomitant authority and support from his superior officers to meet those responsibilities.

In the army Clayton made "command" decisions. In politics his style was similar; he simply was not a "consensus" politician. In combat the opponent was the "the enemy." As a political leader, Clayton often identified the opposite party and even competing factions within his own party as "the enemy." Such an attitude was indeed characteristic of late nineteenth-century politics in the United States and was reinforced by Clayton's own military experience. In war the victor captured contraband from the enemy. In politics, Clayton accepted the legitimacy of the slogan, "To the victor belong the spoils" (of patronage)—another nineteenth-century political concept.

Because Powell Clayton fought in Arkansas with the conquering Union armies and was himself involved in the assault on the state capital and military occupation of the state, he was ever after associated with those events. Indeed, politicians from the "other side of the aisle" often called his party the "Reconstruction Party." Clayton helped organize the Arkansas Republican Party and was its dominant figure for more than three decades. Detractors, therefore, saved their choicest epithets for him. For generations of Democrats, Clayton was nothing less then the *bête noire* of Arkansas politics.

General Clayton retained his military title the rest of his life. He had achieved much in his army career and was proud of it, as his habitual "military bearing" indicated—a perception that affected his personality and his relationships with his family and acquaintances.

Notes

[1]*Daily Times* (Leavenworth, Kansas), 25 January 1859 to 18 August 1859 *passim*.

[2]Albert Castel, *A Frontier State at War: Kansas, 1861-1865* (Ithaca, NY: American Historical Association, 1958). Rev. J.D. Liggett to the A.H.M.S., Leavenworth, 3 December 1862 quoted in Emory Lindquist, "Religion in Kansas During the Era of the Civil War," *Kansas Historical Quarterly*, XXV (1959), 324. *Daily Times* (Leavenworth), August 1859 to January 1861.

[3]Jesse A. Hall *et al.*, *History of Leavenworth County, Kansas* (Topeka: Historical Publishing, 1921). H. Miles Moore, *Early History of Leavenworth City and County* (Leavenworth: Samuel Dodsworth Book Company, 1906). *Collections of Kansas State Historical Society, 1911-1912*, Volume XII (Topeka: Kansas State Printing Office, 1912).

[4]Castel, *Frontier State*. Jay Monaghan, *Civil War on the Western Border, 1854-1865* (New York: Bonanza Books, 1955). Stephen Z. Starr, *Jennison's Jayhawkers: A Civil War Cavalry Regiment and Its Commander* (Baton Rouge: LSU Press, 1973). *Early History Leavenworth*.

[5]Castel, *Frontier State*. Monaghan, *Western Border*. "Military History of Kansas Regiments" in *Report of the Adjutant General of the State of Kansas*, Volume I (Topeka: Kansas State Printing, 1896). Wendell H. Stephenson, *The Political Career of General James H. Lane* (Topeka: Publications of the Kansas State Historical Society, 1930), 128.

[6]*Daily Times*, 4 September 1860 to 9 June 1861 *passim*.

[7]*Ibid*.

[8]Edwin C. Bearss, "Marmaduke Attacks Pine Bluff," *Arkansas Historical Quarterly*, XXIII (1964), 292-94. Photo, 294. Unnamed newspaper clippings, n.d., located in Department of State, Appointment Papers, National Archives, Record Group 59. Undated article entitle "Powell Clayton," Arkansas History Commission, Little Rock, 2. *The War of the Rebellion: A Compilation of the Official Records of the Union and Confederate Armies* (70 vols. in 128, Washington, 1880-1901), ser. I, vol. III, pt. I, 82-83. (Hereafter cited as Official Records.) *Kansas Adjutant General's Office, Military History of Kansas Regiments During the War for the Suppression of the Great Rebellion.* (Leavenworth: W. S. Burke, 1870.) Micropublished in *Western Americana: Frontier History of*

the *Trans-Mississippi West, 1550-1900*. (New Haven, CT: Research Publications, Inc., 1975), Reel 294, No. 2948, 108-118.

[9]*Diary of William F. Creitz, Commander of Company A, Fifth Kansas Cavalry, 11 September 1861 to 11 August 1864*. Kansas State Historical Society, Topeka. *Report of the Adjutant General of the State of Kansas, 1861-1865*. Volume I. (Topeka: Kansas State Printing Company, 1896). Gregory Hermon, "Fifth Kansas Cavalry: a Photo Album," *Military Images Magazine*, Volume V, January-February, 1984, 22-24. Monaghan, *Western Border*, chapter XVII. *Daily Times* (Leavenworth), 1-4 Feb. 1862.

[10]Creitz, *Diary*. Elmo Igenthron, *Borderland Rebellion: A History of the Civil War on the Missouri-Arkansas Border* (Branson, MO: The Ozarks Mountaineer, 1980), 196-209, 283-85.

[11]*Ibid.* Michael Fellman, *Inside War: The Guerrilla Conflict in Missouri During the American Civil War* (New York: Oxford UP, 1989).

[12]Bobby L. Roberts, "General T. C. Hindman and the Trans-Mississippi District," *Arkansas Historical Quarterly*, XXXII (1973), 297-311.

[13]Undated article entitled "Powell Clayton," Arkansas History Commission, Little Rock, 2. *The War of the Rebellion: A Compilation of the Official Records of the Union and Confederate Armies* (70 vols. in 128, Washington, 1880-1901), ser. I, Vol. III, pt. I, 82-83. ser. I, vol. XXII, pt. I, 384-93. vol. XLVIII, pt. II, 429. Creitz, *Diary*.

[14]*Official Records*, ser. I, vol. XXII, pt. I, 236-37, 393-405. Edwin C. Bearss, "The Battle of Helena, July 4, 1863," *Arkansas Historical Quarterly*, XX (1961), 278, 289. Creitz, *Diary*.

[15]*Official Records*, ser. I, vol. XXII, pt. I, 476-77, 486-87, 496-99; pt. II, 674, 1042-43. Bearss, "Pine Bluff," 292-93. *Official Records*, ser. I, vol. XXII, pt. II 723-30. *Official Records*, ser. I, vol. XXXIV, pt. I, 770. *Official Records*, ser. I, vol. XXXIV, pt. I, 660-61, 766-73.

[17]*Official Records*, ser. I, vol. XXXIV, pt. I, 661-65. David O. Demugh, "Federal Military Activity in Arkansas in the Fall of 1864 and the Skirmish at Hurricane Creek," *Arkansas Historical Quarterly*, XXXVIII (1979), 131-45. Ira Don Richards, "The Engagement at Marks' Mills," *Arkansas Historical Quarterly*, XIX (1960), 51-61. Ludwell H. Johnson, *Red River Campaign: Politics and Cotton in the Civil War*. (Baltimore: Johns Hopkins Press, 1958.) Ira Don Richards, "The Battle of Poison Spring," *Arkansas Historical Quarterly*, XVIII (1959), 338-49. James M. Williams to William S. Whitten, 24 April 1864, *Official Records*, Ser. I, Vol. XXXIV, Pt. 1, 746.

[18]*Official Records*, ser. I, Vol. XLI, pt. II, 42-45; vol. XXXIV, pt. III 608-17. Harry S. Ashmore, *Arkansas: A Bicentennial History* (Nashville: American Association for State and Local History, 1978), 86. Monaghan, *Civil War*.

[19]*Official Records*, ser. I, vol. XLI, pt. II, 357, 878; vol. XLVIII, pt. II, 429.

Powell and Adaline Clayton

Chapter Two

GOVERNOR CLAYTON

While still the commanding officer at Pine Bluff, Powell Clayton invited his twin brothers, William and John, also Union veterans, to purchase a plantation with him and settle near Pine Bluff. On 14 December 1865 Powell married Adaline McGraw of Helena, Arkansas, the daughter of a steamboat captain who had served as a major in the Confederate Army.

Clayton was not at first involved in politics and had Unionist friends in both parties. At first he tended to side with President Andrew Johnson against Congress, but declined an offer from a group of Pine Bluff citizens to run as a Congressional candidate on the Democratic ticket. Arkansans usually identified themselves politically as Whigs, Democrats, or states-rights Unionists. Union sentiment was strong in parts of Arkansas, particularly in the northwest, but no Republican party existed there.[1]

After the federal occupation of Little Rock in 1863, the Confederate state government continued to function, exercising some jurisdiction south of the Arkansas River. North of the river Unionist delegates from twenty-two counties met and wrote the Arkansas Constitution of 1864 under which state and local officials were elected. That constitution changed little in the state's political system except that it nullified secession and all political acts of the Arkansas government under the Confederacy. It did not enfranchise blacks. President Lincoln approved the document and the electorate accepted it. Isaac Murphy, a Unionist from Huntsville, was elected governor in 1864. The Civil War ended in April 1865, and the State of Arkansas was re-united under one state government. Democrats, many of them ex-Confederates, captured the state legislature in 1866 and were openly hostile to Unionist Governor Isaac Murphy, even voting pensions for ex-Confederate soldiers almost unanimously over the governor's veto. Though never going beyond the committee stage, a resolution was introduced expressing gratitude to Jefferson Davis for "the noble and patriotic manner in which he conducted the affairs of our government" while he was President of the Confederate States of America. The legislature began using its impeachment powers to purge the state judiciary. In brief, the pro-Confederate majority in Arkansas was in the process of eliminating Unionist control.

When the Arkansas legislature sent two United States Senators to Washington, the Republican-controlled Senate refused to accept them, and in March 1867 Congress declared the governments of Arkansas and nine other former Confederate states illegal. Congressional reconstruction then divided the South into military districts, and the military governor for Arkansas disbanded the Arkansas legislature and called for another constitutional convention.

Meanwhile, Clayton and 138 others organized a Republican state party in Arkansas. Powell Clayton was chosen as the Republican gubernatorial nominee, and James M. Johnson, a native Arkansas unionist, was the Republican candidate for lieutenant governor.

The Democratic state convention of 1868 opposed the new constitution primarily because it included Negro suffrage. It passed a resolution endorsing "a white man's government in a white man's country" and condemned the "forced equality of the races." The convention affirmed its belief in "civil rights" for blacks, but not voting rights. In the first election campaign under the constitution of 1868 Democrats temporarily adopted the political strategy of non-involvement. Since they denied the constitutionality of Congressional reconstruction and wanted to leave the existing system intact, they nominated no one for state office. The result, of course, was a Republican-dominated state government.

The Democratic *Arkansas Gazette* charged the Republican party of Arkansas with favoring "social equality for the Negro and the inter-marriage of the races." A delegate warned that enfranchising blacks was "tantamount to inviting them 'to marry their daughters, and if necessary, hug their wives.'" The *Gazette* urged white Arkansans to desert the Republican party: "White men of Arkansas! Can you longer affiliate with the advocates of miscegenation and mongrelism?"

Though vitriolic political battles were common in Arkansas history, the campaign over ratification of the Constitution of 1868 was more violent than most. Union Leagues, Republican Clubs, Democratic Clubs, and the Ku Klux Klan "supplemented the usual campaign activities," as one historian expressed it. Clayton and other leading Republicans stumped the state, charging Democrats with intimidation and proclaiming loyalty, freedom, Negro rights, and free public education for all. Democrats responded with slander, ridicule, innuendo, and inflammatory rhetoric, referring to Republicans as "damnable curs."[2]

The state board of election commissioners announced ratification of the constitution, and Powell Clayton was inaugurated as Governor of Arkansas on 2 July 1868. Congress declared Arkansas "reconstructed" and granted it representation in Congress. The new Arkansas legislature disfranchised many former Confederates by requiring a loyalty oath before registering to vote.[3]

With the Republicans in control of both the legislative and executive branches of government, the governor was the key figure in the Arkansas political structure. His powers included control over state credit to railroads and patronage appointments, especially of tax assessors and voting registrars. He filled vacancies in state, county, and local offices and appointed many county officials. Competent administrator that he was, Governor Clayton saw the political problems facing his unpopular administration. He realized the value of patronage in maintaining political control of the state and personal control of the party. Early in his administration he sent a letter to all state tax assessors whom he had appointed. After urging them to see that "a fair and correct assessment" was made, Clayton added:

> [The Governor] hopes too that you will look after the interest of the party and keep him informed from time to time in reference to the political situation in your county. He trusts that you will do all you can for the party. He would be pleased if you would make out at your leisure and send to him a list of the prominent Republicans in your county.[4]

Governor Clayton's first nine months in office were a time of violence in Arkansas. Democrats sought to undermine, if not overthrow, what they considered an unconstitutional usurpation of lawful authority by the "Reconstruction Party" then in power. Violence, however, was no stranger to Arkansas. During the war much of the mountain country was in a state of anarchy. Desperados, bushwhackers, and guerrillas wandered about the countryside at will, preying on the scattered populace. Union troops were not stationed in the north in strength and could do little to protect the citizens of the area. Hundreds of people emigrated from the state during the war. The situation was so bad in 1864 that the Murphy government, with the backing of the legislature, requested President Lincoln to send all Arkansas troops then in the United States Army to help the governor "hunt out the marauding bands of thieves and robbers . . . infesting the state." Governor Murphy asked authority from President Lincoln to organize the "Arkansas Rangers," who were to serve in their home districts under officers approved by the governor and who were to be armed and supplied at the expense of the federal government. Secretary of War Edwin Stanton refused the request.[5]

In May 1866 a Northern visitor to Pine Bluff reported that he had seen "Negroes cabbens" on fire and investigated the scene the next morning. "I saw a sight," he wrote, "that apald me 24 Negro men women and children were hanging to trees all around the cabbens."[6]

The Ku Klux Klan crossed the river from Tennessee into Arkansas in the early spring of 1868 and the *Arkansas Gazette* encouraged its formation. In an 18 March 1868 article the *Gazette* credited the Tennessee Klan with generating terror among the "Radicals" who were attempting to "enforce the political and social equality of the African." Although normally deploring secret political organizations, the *Gazette* thought that the times warranted such measures until "a free and just government of the white race" was restored to the South. The *Gazette* continued:

> It has always been and ever will be that where despotism bears cruel sway men will unite themselves for resistance to it and be prepared to avail themselves of opportunities that may offer to overthrow it.[7]

Notices appeared on street corners in Little Rock on 2 April 1868 announcing a Klan meeting that night "at their Grotto, on Beaver Avenue." Similar notices were posted in Pine Bluff and in Batesville, where the editor of the Democratic *North Arkansas Times* warned of the potential danger in such an organization. "We see no reason," he wrote, "why a good, peaceable and orderly citizen should connect himself with any such organization." The Klan reached Fort Smith in April and Arkadelphia in May. By the end of May, the federal commander in Arkansas reported that the Klan "serve their mysterious notices and make their midnight rounds" throughout much of Arkansas. United States troops, numbering only 1,500 in Arkansas, tried to keep some check on Klan activities from twenty-three different locations in the state, but obviously could do little. Democratic newspapers barraged federal troops with criticism for their presence and abused them verbally when they made arrests for Klan activities. The commanding general suggested martial law.[8]

When the new Arkansas government was instituted under the Constitution of 1868 and recognized by Congress, responsibility for maintaining order returned to the civil authorities, and federal troops were limited to nine locations, with the largest concentrations in Little Rock and Fort Smith. Immediately after his inauguration, Governor Clayton requested legislative authorization and funding for the organization of a state guard or militia. Clayton believed strongly that his primary responsibility as Chief Executive of the state was to maintain public order and apprehend those guilty of violent crimes, and he demonstrated vigorous leadership in meeting those duties. The legislature promptly complied with his requests and the Governor issued a proclamation calling for volunteer militiamen. Many Arkansans responded, especially from white northwestern Arkansas and from the black southeast.

Reacting to reports of armed confrontations between groups of black and white citizens in Lewisburg in Conway County, Governor Clayton, without an armed escort, chartered a boat and took with him a bi-partisan group of leading politicians (including future governors Ozro A. Hadley, a Republican, and Augustus H. Garland, a Democrat). In a speech before citizens of Lewisburg, the governor sought to avoid violence through peaceful persuasion but expressed his determination to enforce the election laws.

Random murders continued, mostly of blacks and of white Republicans. Terrorism and intimidation continued to proliferate in various parts of the state. In Crittenden County, across the river from Memphis, the local Freedmen's Bureau agent reported that the Klan consisted of ninety armed men who intended to take over the county by systematic assassination of Republican politicians. In August the agent was shot and wounded. In Mississippi County a gang murdered a member of the legislature, killed six freedmen, and assaulted others. Some county officials were too intimidated to take office. As fall elections approached, the Klan sought to disrupt voter registration of potential Republican voters, particularly among blacks. The most violent continued to be the southern and northeastern counties where lawless bands had long existed.[9]

In Hot Springs the registrar asked for protection and, receiving none, closed his books and refused to register voters. In Drew County a deputy sheriff and a black citizen were murdered, tied together, and left in the road as a macabre warning to others. Two black ministers were beaten and others threatened, one of whom received this letter:

> Sir, We the people have hered that you was a radical. We the party request to no what ticket you intend to vote. If you intend to vote the Democratic ticket if so you can live in our county; if you vote the radical ticket you will not live twenty-four hours, we will kill you as sher as Hell. We the Party.[10]

Missouri militiamen crossed into Arkansas and forced a sheriff to release to their custody four prisoners accused of murder. Hundreds of armed Arkansans from neighboring counties moved to repel the "invasion." Judge Elisha Baxter intervened and secured the release of the prisoners, one of whom was killed, and Governor Clayton swore into Arkansas state service the detachment of Missouri militia and avoided open warfare. Registrars in Sharp and Greene counties resigned. A member of the state legislature was killed. D. P. Upham, Brigadier General of Arkansas state troops, was shot.[11]

Governor Clayton sought to infiltrate the Ku Klux Klan. He found twelve secret service agents from outside the state, some of whom were former Confederates. Those agents produced evidence and *modus operandi* data which helped to suppress the Klan. One of the agents, however, Albert H. Parker, was murdered by the local Klan in White County, northeast of Little Rock. He knew enough Klan ritual and passwords to be admitted to the den in Searcy. Posing as a cattle-buyer, though, he aroused suspicion when he never purchased any cattle. Leaders of the local Klan ordered his execution, and one of their group lured him into a trap where he was surrounded, taken to an isolated farmhouse, and killed. The next day an editorial appeared in the local newspaper claiming that Parker had left the hotel without paying his bill and conjectured that since he was a good Democrat, the Loyal League must have had something to do with his disappearance.

Clayton did not learn of the murder until several months later, when one of the murderers, bothered by a guilty conscience, confessed. Clayton immediately ordered Adjutant Keyes Danforth to take a detail of the Governor's Guard and arrest those involved. Despite efforts by the White County sheriff and his posse to prevent them, Danforth arrested three of those implicated and managed to get them to Little Rock where the governor personally participated in their interrogation. One of the affidavits given by the prisoners included the interesting admission that the members of the Klan had all sworn to "forever oppose the Radical party" and "to place Democrats in power throughout the South." "The object," the Klansman said, was "to carry the elections, and to overturn the radical government, and when [they] were sufficiently organized," they would have "the reins of government" in their own hands.

Legal delays kept the case off the docket for over a year. When the case finally came to trial in circuit court, the regular judge was absent from the bench and in his place sat the former attorney for two of the defendants. The prosecuting attorney moved for a continuance since none of his witnesses were present, but the temporary judge overruled him and, because of insufficient evidence against them, all the accused were acquitted. Clayton, many years later, wrote that he greatly regretted not having declared martial law in White County so that the accused would have been brought before a military tribunal.[12]

On at least one occasion the Governor himself was the target of assassination. One fall night in 1868 Clayton left his work at the Capitol about midnight and began his customary walk down Markham Street toward home. Feeling fatigued, he stopped by a saloon "to get a stimulant." Having noticed three young men observing him surreptitiously, he was particularly cautious as he stepped from the saloon into the beautiful moonlit night. Hearing running footsteps behind him, Clayton immediately stepped into the dark shadow of a high plank fence and cocked his pistol. His pursuers passed rapidly and Clayton detoured to police headquarters for an armed escort. Arriving home, he was greeted by excited servants who informed him that a horseman who had been watching the governor's house for two hours had just left when three men came running to him. From that time the governor used an armed escort at night.[13]

Suppression of armed violence was more difficult because the governor lacked arms and ammunition. Clayton sought unsuccessfully to borrow arms from other governors and finally sent state agents to purchase weapons, but he could find no steamship company willing to handle the cargo. Clayton then chartered a steamer, the *Hesper*, but it was run aground by another boat, boarded, and the arms confiscated. It would seem that such piracy on an interstate waterway (the Mississippi River near Memphis) would bring in the federal authorities, but it did not. The national government was well aware of what was happening in Arkansas. Yet when Governor Clayton requested the use of government arms stored in the United States arsenal at Little Rock, he was refused. President Andrew Johnson was unsympathetic and Gideon Welles, Secretary of the Navy, was openly hostile. Welles regarded the problem as one of partisan politics, neither criminal nor insurrectionary. He called Clayton's alarm "the unreasonable apprehension of a party leader who feared the people he professed to govern." Secretary of War John Schofield was more receptive to the governor's request and urged the President to arm the Arkansas militia with weapons from the Little Rock arsenal. President Johnson, however, refused to permit the use of federal arms by state troops, despite two hundred violent crimes in the preceding four months, including the murder of United States Congressman James M. Hinds.[14]

Clayton wanted federal troops to protect the voter registration process and elections, preferring to use state militia for emergencies. Apparently the governor expected greater support from the federal military than he received. After a weekend visit to Little Rock, Secretary Schofield's aide advised against opening the arsenal to state militia but stressed that the federal commander was "at all times, ready to act . . . in sustaining the state authorities and has so informed the Governor." On 30 October 1868 the federal commander wrote Clayton:

> Where the Civil authorities and entire communities are so paralyzed and helpless as to allow half a dozen outlaws to stalk through the Country in open day and deliberately murder whom they please with impunity, it is clear that a radical change in the local government is necessary. The Military force at my command, or even a much larger one, could not protect the lives of citizens in such helpless communities without the exercise of absolute Martial law. . . . [sic][15]

Just before the federal elections of 1868 Governor Clayton issued a proclamation rejecting voter registration in a dozen Arkansas counties. Ever since then the notion has been widely accepted in Arkansas that Clayton "threw out" enough votes to give the Republicans the election or else he did not "permit" those counties to vote. For example, a county historian later wrote of the election:

> Ashley County was not permitted to vote in the presidential election of 1868 when Grant was elected because its representatives had voted against the adoption of the constitution of the radical Republicans and the county had voted against its adoption. This was done by the governor's setting aside the registration of voters. . . . [16]

Another historian suggested that citizens of the county prevented the election more than the governor. Clayton blamed vigilantes for preventing registration by forcing registering officers in twelve counties to resign, thus making it impossible to hold lawful elections there. Some have seen the governor's actions as an example of his astuteness: unable to prevent the disruption of the election process in those counties, Clayton simply outmaneuvered his opponents. In effect, Clayton permitted the quieter parts of the state to determine the election results.

On 4 November 1868, the day after the federal election, Governor Clayton declared martial law in ten Arkansas counties (later increased to fourteen), proclaiming them in a state of insurrection where the civil authority was "utterly powerless to preserve order and to protect the lives of the citizens." County officers had been killed or intimidated in the performance of their duties. The registration laws had been set aside and a veritable "reign of terror" existed. A few days later the governor went before the legislature to justify his actions and asked for legislative authority and appropriations for the expense of martial law. He summarized the reports reaching his office and declared:

> We are in the midst of civil commotion. . . .
> The element opposed to the government has become so much emboldened as to assume offensive operations and to attempt the overthrow of the

lawful authority in the state. A deep-laid conspiracy was organized for this purpose, and the object was to be accomplished partly by the instrumentality of
the treasonable organization . . . which included in its programme of operations assassinations, robberies, threats, and intimidations. . . .

The governor as commander-in-chief of the militia organized Arkansas into four military districts and named three legislators as commanders: General Robert F. Catterson, Colonel Samuel W. Mallory, and
General D. P. Upham. Clayton did not appoint a commander for the
unionist northwest since it was least affected by vigilante activities. Enough
Arkansas citizens responded to the governor's call that he was able to put
together an effective force. Most volunteers supplied their own weapons
and many rode their own horses. Provisions were supplied by foraging and
commandeering from local citizens, supposedly paid for by vouchers issued
upon the state treasury.

General Catterson assembled his command on 13 November 1868
at Murfreesboro, ninety miles southwest of Little Rock, and sent one
hundred guardsmen into Center Point to seize arms and ammunition stored
there. The mission was successful, but he was soon opposed by some four
hundred armed citizens from nearby counties. A skirmish followed but the
militia held the town, sustaining only six casualties. The troops took
several prisoners and confiscated Ku Klux Klan paraphernalia. Catterson
sought to arrest those accused of major crimes, and a military court ordered
two outlaws hanged.[17]

Though tales of militia depredations were grossly exaggerated by
many who were eager to believe the worst, some of them were true despite
efforts to enforce discipline among the troops. For example, in Sevier
County a group of black militiamen robbed a man's home while one of
them assaulted his wife. General Catterson brought the accused to trial
and the rapist, with Governor Clayton's approval, was publicly executed
by a firing squad of black militiamen. The others involved were dishon-
orably discharged.

Plundering and disorder were more prevalent in Colonel Mallory's
southeastern district, but within only a few weeks many of the militiamen
were mustered out of the service after a large delegation of citizens from
both parties assured the governor of their ability to keep peace. In December Catterson joined Mallory at Monticello and the militia arrested several fugitives, one of whom was executed after a trial before a military
commission. Both groups of militia returned to Little Rock on 5 January
1869.

Meanwhile, General Upham found himself besieged, outnumbered, and outgunned at Augusta, Arkansas. Brazenly, the general took fifteen hostages from among "the leading sympathizers in town" and threatened to kill them and burn the town if his men were attacked. His stratagem worked. Representatives from the town went out to the besiegers and persuaded them to go home.[18]

Eventually the governor ended martial law in exchange for promises of local citizens to maintain order. Despite widespread hostility toward Governor Clayton and the Republican Party, most Arkansas citizens wanted no part of murder. Violence unsettled their lives and most wanted to be left alone by both the Klan and the militia. A number of young Klan members, sickened by what they saw, became disenchanted with what had seemed adventurous a short time earlier. Concerned citizens met in "peace meetings" to urge the governor to revoke martial law with the assurance that they would actively aid in the prevention of unlawful and violent acts. On 21 March 1869, four months after imposing military rule, the governor went before the General Assembly announcing the revocation of martial law. His message included the following statement:

> Repeated assurances have been received from the sheriffs and other offices in those counties that the people are not only willing but desirous to see a faithful and prompt administration of justice in their midst, and to bring all offenders to punishment. The feeling of terrorism and insecurity that existed so generally before the inauguration of martial law has almost entirely disappeared. . . .[19]

In four months had the governor really been able to work such a transformation from anarchy to law and order—with some two thousand militia? Or had the need for martial law been overstated in the first place? On the other side, had "Klayton's Klan" actually brought on the state all the misfortunes it was charged with by those who sought to regain political power, which they believed had been wrested from them by unconstitutional force? One wonders to what extent the political opposition believed its own propaganda, an eloquent illustration of which appeared in the *Gazette* as early as 18 September 1868:

> What is it the Radical party has not done to make every decent Southern man hate, loathe, and abhor every single member of that party? . . . What have they done? Go to the squalid homes of those who once revelled in every luxury that heart could wish and hear their children beg for bread, and ask them who has done this? The sorrow-stricken mother, with tear-bedewed cheek and voice stifled by heartbroken sobs, will tell you, "The Radical party." Go to the once busy marts of trade and see the merchants, mechanics, and artisans lounging about their doors waiting for trade and work, and ask them what has caused

this great change in the business aspect of their city, and they will tell you, "The Radical party." Go to the farmer, and ask him why his once blooming fields are lying in waste and uncultivated, and he will tell you, "Because of the ruinous policy of the Radical party." Go to your treasuries, state and national, look into their empty vaults, and ask their keepers what has become of the gold which inclined them, and if they would tell you truly, they would say, "Squandered by the Radical party." Ask the head of the treasury department who created this mountain of debt under which the government now groans, and he will tell you, "The Radical party." Go to the polls, see the illiterate and ignorant negroes jostling away our most worthy and intelligent white men, and ask who has done this, and the answer will be, "The Radical party.". . . All these wrongs, aye! a thousand times more, have that party heaped upon the South, and yet they have the unblushing effrontery to ask us to treat them as friends and associates. As well take into our bosom the poisonous adder or into our houses a rabid dog as to cultivate terms of sociality and friendship with these vampires upon the body politic—these despoilers of the rights and liberties of our people. . . ![20]

Editorials such as this one helped create the folklore of the terror of "Clayton's militia." That thousands of ordinary citizens believed that the Republican party was responsible for crimes as charged and that Powell Clayton in particular was the chief villain was evident from the scores of letters, court depositions, and other contemporary documents. Embellishment grew with the retelling. An eyewitness to Catterson's Battle of Center Point described the events he saw and heard about in a letter written in 1890. He described looting and pillaging by a squad of "armed ragamuffins," reported torture and intimidation by Catterson, and stated that "on the way one of the negro militia raped . . . a most estimable lady who resided near Paraclifta. And yet Clayton still lives!" Such accounts which sought to justify Ku Klux Klan vigilantism and assassinations were more often than not accepted uncritically at face value.[21]

A letter written by a citizen of Arkansas to President Andrew Johnson early in 1869 described various alleged crimes of Catterson's militia, including the charge that they "took two of the quiet old citizens and shot them." The catalog of crimes ended with the illuminating comment that "all of which is done by consent and under order of Gov. Clayton." The uncritical, credulous comment made by the editor of that letter in 1962 is a typical interpretation of the period: "It was these things, happening three years after the close of the Civil War, and not the Civil War itself, that so embittered the people against Powell Clayton and the Republican Party." One suspects that the bitterness was more engendered by the widespread perception of what happened rather than by the events themselves. Opposition newspapers must, then, share the responsibility for the negative public perception, particularly since much of what was printed was obviously false or badly distorted.[22]

There was simply no way that "Clayton's militia" could have carried out the many depredations with which it was charged. That outrages, indignation, robberies, rapes, and even murder did actually occur is probable. There were just too many eyewitness accounts to dismiss all of them as fabrications. Even by making generous allowance for hatred, venom, vindictiveness, emotional embellishment, and even contrived propaganda, it is difficult for the historian to believe that all of the tales were fictitious.

Nevertheless, Governor Clayton was not a tyrant. Moreover, he lacked the means of instituting a tyrannical system. Where was his oppressive program, his blueprint for action? By what means would he implement a dictatorship? Where were the men and money needed to enforce his will? Far from being a dictator, Clayton was merely a politician who sought to administer a minority government in turbulent times.

Did an anti-government conspiracy in fact exist in Arkansas as Governor Clayton contended in his martial law proclamation? The evidence seems conclusive that indeed there was such a conspiracy, centered around the Ku Klux Klan and informally supported by scores of journalists and politicians. Was this an effort to overthrow the state government by force? Probably not, though some of those involved no doubt would have liked to do so, and even considered the Ku Klux Klan organization a rejuvenated Confederate Army. The presence of United States troops in Arkansas silently emphasized the constitutional obligation of the national government to protect the states from "domestic violence."

What was involved, though, was a conspiracy to undermine the authority of the state government and obstruct its effectiveness. In his carefully worded speech on martial law Clayton did not state that a conspiracy existed to overthrow the government, but that a "deep laid conspiracy" was organized for the purpose of attempting "the overthrow of the lawful authority in the State," that is, obstructing the effectiveness of that authority and undermining its legitimacy in the minds of the citizens.

One wonders how much more difficult the task of governing became because of the intemperate language and unrestrained rhetoric used by the Democratic press of Arkansas, particularly by the *Arkansas Gazette*. A bit of embellishment for propaganda purposes may be overlooked by the critical observer, but deliberately to attempt to undermine the authority of the existing government through distortions, fabrications, and character assassination showed no respect either for the person involved or for the political process itself. Ideas led to action, and ideas and attitudes were presumably affected by what one read and discussed. What excuse, for example, could the editor of the *Gazette* have for referring to the governor and his staff as "Powell Clayton and his pimps"?[23]

The press, of course, was an effective tool to undermine any sense of legitimacy that citizens of Arkansas might feel for the existing government. Many, no doubt, sincerely believed that their constitutional rights were being violated by franchise restrictions, but surely this journalist must have had little regard for truth when he wrote:

> The rule of the radicals in this state . . . has been one continuous and outrageous orgy of corruption and crime. . . . No age, no country, no people have suffered what is here described. . . . This is no longer a party question. It is a question of right and wrong. It matters not now if the governor or the so-called governor Clayton is governor of Arkansas, or a mere leader of guerrillas. Before God and man, by the acts of his myrmidons, he has rendered himself amenable for murders and outrages that should consign him to capital punishment on earth and whatever punishment is in store for the wicked elsewhere.[24]

Certainly the Clayton administration was not the only target of the journalists' bludgeon. In May 1870, the *Gazette* libeled a circuit court judge, John Whytock, who found both editors guilty of contempt and threw one of them in jail for five days. The decision was upheld by the Arkansas Supreme Court, claiming that all courts inherently had the power "to preserve their dignity and respect for their authority" against those "who by any conduct attempt to poison or prejudice the public mind against the dignity and authority of such tribunals." Nevertheless, the *Gazette* thundered back:

> . . . Contempt! If every man who holds the little ass . . . in ineffable contempt were subjected to the same punishment, a thousand county jails could not hold them. . . . John Whytock, the malignant, . . . [is] as innocent of law as he is any other learning. . . .[25]

The *Gazette* was hostile to Clayton from the beginning of his gubernatorial career. It applauded and defended the *Hesper* piracy; made light of the "dreadful" Ku Klux Klan; and hoped that the lieutenant governor would arrest the "absconding governor" for "fraudulent and treasonable practices." When the *White River Journal* commended Governor Clayton for his courage, surrounded as he was with hostility and more problems to contend with than "usually falls the lot of anyone," the *Gazette* disagreed, claiming Clayton was against the "poor, down-trodden, broken-hearted people of Arkansas."[26]

The Helena *Shield* reported the governor's visit to ease dissension among Republicans:

> The governor's reception here last Sunday morning was a stunning affair. The diminutive, one-boiler, low-priced, fourth class stern wheel steamboat, that brought this pompous specimen of official arrogance around, arrived here at 9 o'clock, and on placing his official foot upon Phillips county soil, he was met by Jerry, the porter of the Shelby House. . . .[27]

One suspects that much of this rhetoric was calculated to manipulate and entertain. When Governor Clayton suffered the painful loss of his hand in a hunting accident, the *Gazette* was gracious in its response:

> We learn with sincere regret that Governor Clayton met with a sad accident on Saturday last, which resulted in the loss of his left hand. He had gone into the country on a shooting occasion and while endeavoring to draw a load from his gun a cap exploded and the contents were lodged in his hand. The wound was a terrible one and amputation was found necessary. While regretting this serious casualty, it affords us pleasure to state that the governor is comparatively easy and that his recovery promises to be speedy.

A few weeks later the *Gazette* thought Clayton had "a sort of liberality and suavity of manner that attracted to him many warm personal friends." He was, however, a "little man" with a "narrow mind."[28]

The image of Clayton as a tyrant has persisted in Arkansas, perpetuated in part by Democratic dominance in the state, but if the political struggle during Reconstruction in Arkansas centered on the issues of legitimacy, stability, and order, then Governor Clayton showed decisive and forceful leadership in establishing martial law. When local citizens accepted their responsibility to support local officials in maintaining order, such a drastic measure as military rule was no longer necessary. Four months was long enough for the governor to make his point.

Other historians have reached similar conclusions:

> Governor Powell Clayton's . . . policy of military arrests, trials, and executions constituted the only successful resistance to the Klan that occurred anywhere in the Reconstruction South. . . .[29]

And a specialist on the Ku Klux Klan concluded:

> It seems very clear now as it did then that the militia campaign was directly responsible for disrupting the Klan and restoring peace throughout most of Arkansas. Governor Clayton's calculated risk had paid off. As a result he ac-

complished more than any other Southern governor in suppressing the Ku Klux conspiracy.[30]

If the Republican administration of Arkansas had great difficulties governing the state, the governor also had trouble leading his own party. Clayton apparently did not see much difference between loyalty to the party and loyalty to Powell Clayton and was soon faced with an intra-party split. Clayton sought to lead his party as he had commanded his regiment. Resentment followed, of course, especially when he distributed patronage primarily to develop personal loyalty to himself. Opposition to the regular party organization centered more on personalities than on ideological differences. Intra-party strife surfaced on 8 April 1869 when Lieutenant Governor James Johnson and seventeen state legislators met to organize a new party in opposition to Governor Clayton. The new organization sought to attract the old Whigs of Arkansas who, though Unionists, had never been Nationalists, believing in state and regional autonomy within the Federal Union. They established *The Liberal* as a party newspaper and formally organized the Liberal Republican Party of Arkansas on 14 October 1869 with Joseph Brooks as one of its principal leaders. The new party called for greater economy in government, a reduction of gubernatorial powers, and the immediate enfranchisement of all men. It charged Clayton with criminal abuse of his power as commander-in-chief of the state militia, criminal and corrupt mismanagement of railroad interests through his "unfair distribution of state aid," and extravagant appropriations for the state government.[31]

Unsubstantiated allegations were made from time to time that Governor Clayton had received kickbacks in exchange for approving state aid to certain railroads. Such charges were particularly useful to his opponents because they were vague, sweeping, and difficult to counter. Granting state, local, and federal aid to railroads was an established practice in the United States long before Clayton took office, justified by an appeal to the economic stimulation that railroads brought with them. Clayton and the 1868 legislature which authorized such aid built on the practices of the past. For example, the Democratic legislature preceding Congressional Reconstruction authorized local aid and granted state aid at $10,000 a mile (over Governor Isaac Murphy's veto). Indeed, the *Gazette* in 1870 credited the Democrats with starting the policy of railroad aid: "Our own people," it claimed, "set on foot this spirit of improvement before the cormorants came." The Clayton administration submitted the issue to a popular referendum calling for state bonds of $10,000 per mile for railroads receiving federal land grants and $15,000 per mile for others. The electorate approved the plan almost unanimously.[32]

Thirty-eight miles of railroad were in operation in Arkansas when the Civil War began, but no track was laid again until 1868. During the Clayton administration 218 miles of railroad were built and another 444 miles during the subsequent Republican administration. By comparison, only 108 miles of track were laid during the rest of the decade, after Democratic control returned in 1874, due partly to the depression of 1873 and partly because of the new state constitutional prohibition against the use of state credit for railroad construction.

Eighty-six companies requested state aid from the Clayton administration. The pattern of approval followed the pre-war design so that only the five railroads following the main arteries received state credit in bonds. All of the assisted railroads eventually defaulted on their payments and the state of Arkansas took possession of them through receivers, leaving the state with payments it was unable to meet.[33]

Clayton was the target of innuendo and rumor rather than of formal charges of wrongdoing in railroad matters. Later Democratic investigations never found evidence to substantiate those insinuations. Indeed, most opponents, in spite of a long list of grievances against Clayton, did not accuse him of financial wrongdoing. Clayton wrote in 1914:

> I was frequently criticized for my actions in connection with the issuance of bonds to aid in the construction of the various railroads and while I was never openly charged with appropriating any of them for my own use, it was strongly hinted that I had been well paid for the aid I had given to the railroads. I will state positively that until the year 1892 when ten of them came into my possession, I had never owned nor held a single bond that had been issued to aid in the construction of railroads.[34]

It is interesting, however, that not long after Clayton's term as governor ended, in 1873 he assumed the presidency of the newly-consolidated Little Rock, Mississippi River, and Texas Railroad Company. Clayton said he accepted the position "very reluctantly" but finally did so because the line ran through his Pine Bluff plantation on ground that he had donated to the railroad.[35]

Another issue of Clayton's administration was his role in budgetary and funding matters. Liberal Republicans and Democrats alike charged him with "extravagance" in spending and fiscal policy. Supporters of the administration credited him and the Arkansas General Assembly with constructive legislation which encouraged social improvement and economic prosperity. The administration was interested in economic growth, immigration, and the development of rail and water transportation systems. State funding of institutions for the blind, deaf, and insane began. Clayton encouraged the passage of the school law of 1868 which brought free public education to blacks for the first time. In the pre-war period of Arkansas history the legislature did not supplement Congressional land endowments for education and Arkansas had a sixty-five percent illiteracy rate. Some private academies existed, but in 1860 only twenty-five common schools were supported from the common school fund, endowed by federal land grants. There were no school taxes in Arkansas.

After the Civil War Governor Isaac Murphy urged the Democratic legislature to establish a free public school system partially supported by property taxes of two mills. The legislature concurred and in 1867 school taxation began in Arkansas. Blacks were exempt from the tax—and from public education, as there was no provision for Negro schools. A Superintendent of Public Instruction was elected and county school commissioners appointed.

Governor Clayton and the Republican legislature retained most of the education law of 1867 but made several significant changes, the most obvious of which was the provision for the education of Negroes—in separate schools from whites. The two-mill property tax continued with a poll tax of one dollar for each male over twenty-one years of age. Compulsory education, though included in the law, was not vigorously enforced. A circuit system of ten superintendents replaced the county superintendent system. Democratic opponents charged the administration with establishing unnecessary political patronage positions paying high salaries. Republicans claimed the system was more efficient and not lucrative when expenses of administering the circuit were taken into consideration.[36]

The constitution of 1868 charged the legislature with the responsibility of establishing a state university. Arkansas received the federal land endowment provided by the Morrill Act and Governor Clayton appointed a state board to locate the university in the region which would subscribe the greatest financial contribution for the institution. Shortly after Clayton's term of office Fayetteville was officially designated as the site for the University of Arkansas.

State funds provided for these new programs, and salaries of state officials increased substantially above pre-war levels. The Clayton administration increased taxes and expanded property subject to taxation. Before the Civil War, hill country land had been assessed at three dollars an

acre, while plantation land was assessed at much less. Republican assessors incurred much hostility in the river counties, including Pulaski County
where Little Rock was located, by a more equal tax assessment. The *Gazette* screamed in pain: "women and young girls [had] to drive the family milch cows through the streets to get money to pay taxes upon [those]
fraudulent assessments and valuations." Interestingly, the publisher of the
Gazette, William E. Woodruff, owned a mansion and twenty-four acres
of land on the outskirts of Little Rock. His property had an assessed value
of twenty-four dollars. At the same time a black mechanic who owned a
small house and two lots in Little Rock received an assessment of eight
hundred dollars. Republicans, of course, cited such examples to justify their
policy, and Clayton directed that no land was to be sold for back taxes until
the owner had an opportunity to redeem it.[37]

Increased taxes, however, did not provide sufficient revenue to
operate the government and the state issued scrip to meet immediate
operating expenses. The value of scrip, of course, deteriorated and most
creditors refused to accept the scrip, which, nevertheless, had to be accepted at par for all tax payment. Consequently, many individuals (including some tax collectors) purchased scrip considerably below par and used
it at par to pay taxes, pocketing the profit. The legislature then instructed
the governor to issue new state bonds at six percent interest to replace
existing bonds in order to retire the current indebtedness of the state.

Paying the pre-war bonded indebtedness of Arkansas, however,
complicated matters. Shortly after admission to the Union as a state in
1836, Arkansas chartered the Bank of Arkansas and the Real Estate Bank,
both of which failed in the Panic of 1837, shackling the state with a debt
it could not pay. Part of that indebtedness was the Holford Bonds, five
hundred $1,000 bonds issued by the state of Arkansas in 1840. Those se-
curities later were sold to Holford and Company, London bankers, for
approximately $121,000. Arkansas refused to redeem the bonds for more
than it had originally received for them on the grounds that the transfer
to the London bankers violated the original agreement made with the
American Trust and Banking Company of New York. The funding act
of 1869 provided for full funding at par including interest. In addition,
the Republican legislature authorized $2,000,000 in levee bonds and rail-
road bonds. By the mid-1870s the government was borrowing short-term
money to meet current expenses. In 1877 and 1878 the Arkansas State
Supreme Court ruled that the railroad bonds and levee bonds had been
issued unconstitutionally. In 1884 the electorate repudiated them and the
Holford bonds.[38]

Clayton was a convenient scapegoat for Arkansas' funding problems. He, of course, had nothing to do with the pre-war debts which his administration inherited. Whether the Holford bonds should have been funded in excess of $121,000 was a moot question, but the law did not permit the governor to reduce the full funding of the old bonds, including the controversial Holford bonds. The Panic of 1873 contributed to the financial collapse of the railroads and the reduction of the necessary tax base to finance the state government. The Democratic administrations of the 1870s were unwilling to raise taxes to pay government expenses and fund bonded indebtedness also. Funding problems were perennial and confronted governors of both political parties. Powell Clayton was neither better nor worse in solving these problems than his political opposition.

Ethical issues of repudiation were obscured in the controversy and the political turmoil of debt repudiation made it difficult for Arkansas to attract needed capital for economic development. If the economy had been more prosperous or the results of state aid more beneficial, it would not have been as easy to use the Republican administration as the scapegoat for Arkansas' economic and social problems.

A rather startling incident occurred in the summer of 1869 when Clayton went to New York on state funding matters without notifying Lieutenant Governor Johnson. When some of Clayton's political enemies learned of his absence from the state, they sent for the Lieutenant Governor, who was at home in northern Arkansas. Johnson was to go immediately to Little Rock to assume the office of governor that Clayton had allegedly "vacated" by leaving the state! The *Gazette* made sport of the occasion:

> Anxious inquiries are being made as to the whereabouts of the governor. . . . If our northern contemporaries see a stray governor up that way will they please inform us? We are very anxious about our executive. The horrible ku-klux are so bad. Where's our governor . . . and the balance of our state government? They are gone—somewhere. *Sic transit gloria klayton klan.*[39]

Clayton hastened back to Little Rock to occupy "the governor's office" as well as "the office of governor" and beat Johnson to Little Rock, thus averting an attempted coup within the state government. Rumors suggested that Lieutenant Governor Johnson might even arrest Governor Clayton and seek his impeachment by the legislature.

Before "sneaking back to his mountain home," as Clayton later wrote, Johnson blasted the governor in a speech to a crowd gathered in front of the Anthony House in Little Rock. He charged that Clayton's faction had assumed the right to "dictate the policy of the party" and had inaugurated a "reign of terror" against party members who dared oppose their "swindling operations." "This mighty man, Powell Clayton, declared war on the people." Why had the governor quietly left the state without informing the lieutenant governor? It was "obvious" to Johnson that "there was something which it was necessary to cover up." He charged Clayton and his associates with corruption in awarding state aid to railroads and funding the state debt.[40]

Such talk from the lieutenant governor was more than mere invective or a maneuver to gain control of the Arkansas Republican Party. Clayton thought it might even endanger his life, since his assassination would put Johnson in the governor's chair. Clayton responded by initiating *quo warranto* proceedings against Johnson, forcing him to show legally how he held his office. That was simply legal harassment and the matter was dropped.

The schism between the governor and the lieutenant governor complicated Clayton's senatorial ambitions. He was elected to the United States Senate by the Arkansas legislature on 10 January 1871 by a large margin, some of it perhaps motivated by the prospect of removing Clayton from the state government and replacing him with Lieutenant Governor Johnson. The legislature elected in 1870 had a larger number of Democrats than its predecessor, so each of the three political factions—Regular Republicans, Liberal Republicans, and Democrats—was more evenly represented. Governor Clayton was not to be eliminated so easily. He wanted to go to the Senate, but not until the governor's office was safe from Johnson. The pro-Clayton faction in the legislature again initiated impeachment proceedings against Johnson, but failed to win a majority.

Finally Clayton demonstrated either a sense of humor (which he often lacked) or his influence in Washington even in those early years by offering Johnson the federal office of minister to the Sandwich Islands, a post which Johnson declined. At this juncture the anti-Clayton forces, composed of Liberal Republicans and Democrats, seized the initiative, bringing impeachment proceedings against Governor Clayton. They charged him with conspiracy to deprive Lieutenant Governor Johnson of his office unlawfully, of directing election frauds, and of misusing his power to issue railroad bonds.

The discussion surrounding the forty-two to thirty-eight vote in the Arkansas House of Representatives was lively. The articles of impeachment included the proviso that Powell Clayton "is hereby suspended from exercising the functions of Governor of the State of Arkansas. . . ." Some objected to that stipulation as being in violation of existing laws regarding impeachments. Others questioned the procedure being used. Still others believed too much credence was given to allegations by Clayton's political enemies. Some thought it peculiar that the same body that had elected Clayton to the United States Senate only a few days earlier should vote to impeach him. Requesting evidence to substantiate the charges against the governor, Clayton's supporters could only get verbal assurances that such evidence did exist. They were, nevertheless, asked to suspend the governor from his office on the basis of those assurances. At least one representative labeled the proceeding a "malicious prosecution" "unjust, unwise, unparliamentary, unprecedented, and revolutionary."[41]

Governor Clayton immediately wrote a letter to the House of Representatives, stating, ". . . I am advised by competent and able legal gentlemen that the Constitution does not confer the power of suspension from office on your honorable body. . . ." The House, however, voted forty-two to thirty-two that "the message just received from Powell Clayton, be not received as a message from the Governor of the State of Arkansas." The next day a legislator presented a resolution to the house to request the President and Congress of the United States "to interpose their power to protect the people of Arkansas from the usurpations of Powell Clayton and his confederates."[42]

Pro-Clayton Arkansas Senators deliberately absented themselves from the Senate in order to prevent the calling of a quorum, without which the House could not legally complete the impeachment. The law stated that the governor was to be suspended from office, not when he was found guilty by the Senate, but when the House had duly informed the Senate of impeachment before the trial was ever held in the Senate. Frustrated by this maneuver, the House committee charged with formally conveying the impeachment resolution to the Senate resigned.

Governor Clayton, seeking to avoid violence, sought relief in the Arkansas Supreme Court. He petitioned Chief Justice John McClure, his personal and political friend, to issue a restraining order on Lieutenant Governor Johnson "from attempting to take possession" of the governor's office. McClure did so until the Senate as a court of impeachment should pass on the articles of impeachment. In spite of the court order, the lieutenant governor made formal demand for Clayton to surrender his office. Clayton refused and the Little Rock *Republican* counseled people to choose sides and be prepared for violence:

> The state government will not be surrendered without a fight; and when it does come, our cry shall be "Lay on Macduff, and damned be he who first cries hold, enough."[43]

The new Board of Managers for the House impeachment, all Democrats, sought to find evidence to substantiate the charges against the governor. Despite assurances of the "abundance and sufficiency of proof at hand," they found almost no evidence. What they did find, the committee considered "entirely inadequate to sustain the charges against the Governor, and too frivolous to attempt a further prosecution" of the case. Consequently the impeachment proceedings were dropped by a vote of forty-nine to six with fifteen abstentions.[44]

Abundant rhetoric and posturing accompanied the voting. One representative suggested that the impeachment charges had been brought by the "meanest set of lick-spittles and Spanish poodles" in Arkansas. Another charged that Clayton's calling out of the militia was "sufficient to eternally damn any man, politically or otherwise."[45]

With impeachment a dead issue, Arkansas Secretary of State Robert J. T. White resigned and Clayton offered to appoint Johnson in his place. Johnson, "now battered and beaten," accepted. White claimed he resigned simply in the interest of party harmony. Others accused the Claytonites of paying him $5,000 in cash and $25,000 in bonds for agreeing to the deal. Later, a special Congressional investigation determined that White had, indeed, received a sum of money for expenses to enable him to return to Virginia. White testified that he had long wanted to leave Arkansas and had merely sold his equity in his business. The legislature again elected Clayton to the United States Senate and the pro-Clayton President of the Arkansas Senate, Ozro A. Hadley, became governor in March 1871.[46]

Powell Clayton's three-year term as governor was a turbulent period. Attacks on him were virulent and scurrilous. Hostility and character assassination characterized much of what was written about Clayton. He was charged with all sorts of infamous and dastardly deeds, from being a dictator motivated by a desire to "humiliate the Southern people" to murdering Arkansas Governor Jeff Davis's aunt. Clayton's enemies would have delighted in finding him criminally guilty of anything. The fact that they never were able to do so is an indication of either his astuteness or his honesty, but the evidence points to the latter. As one historian put it, Clayton "was always a partisan, often an opportunist, but never a thief."[47]

Reconstruction in Arkansas, with its own unique characteristics, was, nevertheless, part of the pattern of events throughout the South. Its meaning and failures are still being debated by historians, but its historical significance is obvious. Powell Clayton was caught in the tension and turmoil of the period and was no more successful in resolving the basic issues than his contemporaries.

The Civil War settled the issue of the indissolubility of the Union and emancipated the slaves. It also expanded the authority of the national government and altered federal-state relations. Reconstruction was a constitutional test of the extent of that change. The South challenged the federal government militarily in the Civil War and the struggle continued politically during Reconstruction. Just as slaves were caught in the middle of the pre-Civil War national debates, newly freed blacks were caught in the political tug-of-war during Reconstruction.

It is too often assumed that the constitutional issues of autonomy or self-rule were merely Southern rationalizations for white supremacy and that Republican championing of political rights for blacks was merely a device to add to their numbers politically. Both sides had emotional principles at stake: black political rights vs. autonomy within the federal union. And both sides had a built-in political self-interest in the issues. Ex-slaves were beholden to the Republicans for their freedom and white Southerners could realize their political dominance only with northern influence removed from the South. But newcomers like Powell Clayton did not consider themselves interlopers or outsiders. Clayton made his home in Arkansas and invested most of his adult life helping to develop the state. He was an opportunist, but he was also a builder. In many ways he typified the political ambivalence and tension of the times.

Notes

[1] Powell Clayton, *The Aftermath of the Civil War in Arkansas* (New York: The Neale Publishing Company, 1915), 30-31.

[2] Powell Clayton to All Tax Assessors, January 24, 1870, *Clayton Letterbook*, Arkansas History Commission, Little Rock.

[3] Clayton, 50. *Arkansas Laws, 1868*, 55, sec. 11.

[4] Powell Clayton to All Tax Assessors, 24 January 1870 *Clayton Letterbook*, Arkansas History Commission, Little Rock.

[5] Otis A. Singletary, "Militia Disturbances in Arkansas During Reconstruction," *Arkansas Historical Quarterly*, XV (1956), 140-150.

[6] J. W. Mallet to Thaddeus Stevens, 28 May 1866, Stevens Papers. Quoted in Richard N. Current, *Those Terrible Carpetbaggers* (New York: Oxford UP, 1988), 135.

[7] *Arkansas Gazette*, 18 March 1868.

[8] *North Arkansas Times* (Batesville), April 18, 1868, in Allen W. Trelease, *White*

Terror: The Ku Klux Klan Conspiracy and Southern Reconstruction (New York: Harper and Row, 1971), 100.

[9]Powell Clayton, *The Aftermath of the Civil War in Arkansas* (New York: The Neale Publishing Company, 1915), 106ff, 144-49.

[10]*Morning Republican* (Little Rock), September 15, 1868. Michael P. Kelley, "Partisan or Protector: Powell Clayton and the 1868 Presidential Election," *The Ozark Historical Review*, III (Spring, 1974), 53.

[11]William Monks, *A History of Southern Missouri and Northern Arkansas* (West Plains, MO: West Plains Journal Company, 1907). Eli H. Mix to Powell Clayton, September 20, 1868, L. C. Gulley Collection, Arkansas History Commission, Little Rock.

[12]Clayton, 84-85.

[13]Clayton, 63-85, 102-105.

[14]Gideon Welles, *Diary of Gideon Welles: Secretary of the Navy under Lincoln and Johnson* (Boston: Houghton Mifflin, 1911), III, 460-61. Clayton, 106ff.

[15]General C. H. Smith to Powell Clayton, October 30, 1868, in Howard C. Westwood, "The Federals' Cold Shoulder to Arkansas' Powell Clayton," *Civil War History*, XXVI (September, 1980), 248.

[16]Y. W. Etheridge, *History of Ashley County Arkansas* (Van Buren, AR, 1959), 112.

[17]Clayton, 63-80, Kelley, 50-55.

[18]*Ibid.*

[19]W. H. H. Clayton to Powell Clayton, January 9, 1914. Clayton, 65-80.

[20]*Arkansas Gazette*, September 18, 1868.

[21]Virginia Buxton, "Clayton's Militia in Sevier and Howard Counties," *Arkansas Historical Quarterly*, XX (1961), 345-48.

[22]W. H. Reid, Robert McKinney, and William Joiner to Andrew Johnson, January 12, 1869, in J. H. Atkinson, ed., "Clayton and Catterson Rob Columbia County," *Arkansas Historical Quarterly*, XXI (1962), 153-57.

[23]*Arkansas Gazette*, February 23, 1871.

[24]*Pine Bluff Weekly Press*, March 25, 1869, *The Arkansas Gazette*, January 3, 1869.

[25]*Arkansas Gazette*, June 14, 1870.

[26]*Arkansas Gazette*, February 13, 1869.

[27]Quoted in *The Arkansas Gazette*, August 16, 1870.

[28]*Arkansas Gazette*, September 10, October 13, 1868.

[29]Otto H. Olsen, ed., *Reconstruction and Redemption in the South* (Baton Rouge: LSU Press, 1980), 181.

[30]Trelease, 174.

[31]Orval T. Driggs, Jr., "The Issues of the Powell Clayton Regime, 1868-1871," *Arkansas Historical Quarterly*, VIII (Spring, 1949), 1-75 passim., Staples, 375-78.

[32]Carter Goodrich, "Public Aid to Railroads in the Reconstruction South," *Political Science Quarterly*, LXXI (September, 1956), 425-26. *The Arkansas Gazette*, September 15, 1870.

[33]Goodrich, 436.

[34]Clayton, 249.

[35]Clayton, 247.

[36]Charles William Dabney, *Universal Education in the South* (Chapel Hill: North Carolina UP, 1936), I, 381-92 passim. Robert C. Morris, *Reading, 'Riting, and Reconstruction: The Education of Freedmen in the South, 1861-1870* (Chicago: U of Chicago P, 1981), 244-45.

[37]*Arkansas Gazette*, August 8, 1869.

[38]Bessie Carter Randolph, "Foreign Bondholders and the Repudiated Debts of the Southern States," *American Journal of International Law*, XXV (January, 1931), 63-82 *passim*. William Clarence Evans, "The Public Debt of Arkansas: Its History from 1836 to 1885," unpublished M.A. thesis, University of Arkansas, 1928, *passim*.

[39]*Arkansas Gazette*, July 17, 1869; July 23, 1869. *Sic transit gloria klayton klan*="Thus passes away the glory of the klayton klan."

[40]Staples, 377.

[41]Arkansas General Assembly, *Proceedings in the House of Representatives of Arkansas in the Case of the Impeachment of Governor Powell Clayton*. (Little Rock: Price and Barton, 1871,) 4.

[42]*Ibid*. Cortez A. M. Ewing, "Arkansas Reconstruction Impeachments," *Arkansas Historical Quarterly*, XIII (1954), 137-53.

[43]*Ibid*. *Little Rock Republican*, February 19, 1871. (A later Democratic-controlled House brought impeachment charges against the Chief Justice for this action, but the charges were dismissed by a 19-3 vote of the Senate.)

[44]*Proceedings House of Representatives*, 30-31.

[45]*Ibid*., 54.

[46]Driggs, 71. Staples, 385-87.

[47] Mark W. Summers, *Railroads, Reconstruction, and the Gospel of Prosperity: Aid Under the Radical Republicans, 1865-1877* (Princeton, NJ: Princeton UP, 1984), 248-49.

Chapter Three

SENATOR CLAYTON

Powell Clayton's senatorial career began, as with so much of his public life, with a rousing send-off by admiring well-wishers and a less-than-cordial farewell by the *Arkansas Gazette*. As a band played "Shoo Fly," his train pulled away from the station, taking Governor Clayton to Washington, according to the *Gazette*, "to misrepresent the people and degrade the honor and dignity of Arkansas" in the United States Senate.

Senator Clayton scrupulously observed the tradition of freshmen senators by assuming a quiet, supportive role. He served on four minor committees. During his second session Clayton was the subject of a sena-torial investigation initiated by the Senator himself. The 21 December 1871 Washington *Chronicle* reported "War Declared Against Senator Clayton." "Several prominent gentlemen from Arkansas" had just arrived in Washington "for the purpose of having Senator Clayton expelled" from the United States Senate. At the time, indictments were pending in Ar-kansas charging former Governor Clayton with having issued a certificate of election to the United States House of Representatives to John Edwards, a Democrat, instead of to Thomas Boles, his Republican opponent. The charges alleged that Clayton had agreed to issue the certificate in exchange for Democratic votes in the Arkansas legislature for his election to the United States Senate. The indictments were soon dropped, but the Sen-ate gave Clayton several hours to explain the matter in detail. Far from Democratic votes contributing to his "handsome majority" in the Arkan-sas legislature, Clayton insisted that only one Democrat voted for him in either house. That single vote puzzled him, but he thought it was perhaps because the Democrat was "a Methodist preacher and a conscientious man."

Arkansas had a peculiar election law which provided that if the law-ful judges of election failed to appear at the appointed time to open the polling place in a precinct, then the waiting voters could elect their own election officials! Clayton explained that in Pulaski county certain indi-viduals in several precincts prevented the judges from opening the polls and took charge of them themselves. In other precincts two polls were set up. In the election in question the Arkansas Supreme Court concluded that only the elections held by the judges appointed by the board of registration were legal. The Arkansas legislature also investigated the election and agreed with the Supreme Court. Clayton as chief executive thought it wise to accept the judgment of the other two branches of government. He then certified the Democrat as the lawfully elected Congressman.

Clayton concluded his lengthy speech by requesting the appointment of a special committee to report on the allegations against him. The Senate unanimously agreed, but a year passed before the committee finished its reports. The investigation, of course, occupied much of Clayton's time and energy. Meanwhile the committee of the House of Representatives investigating the same election concluded that, despite the disputed returns, Republican Thomas Boles was entitled to the Congressional seat. Edwards was upset that the decision of the Arkansas Supreme Court and the Arkansas Assembly had no bearing on the matter, but the United States Constitution gave exclusive power to each house in such disputes.[2]

The Senate Committee investigating "Certain Allegations Against Honorable Powell Clayton" examined thirty-eight witnesses from January to May, 1872. At the end of the session its preliminary report sparked several scathing exchanges on the Senate floor. Clayton had already clashed with Francis P. Blair, Jr., Senator from Missouri, and did so again. Senator Thomas Bayard of Delaware observed that the House of Representatives had given the Congressional seat to Boles rather than Edwards, thus implying that Clayton's action was "a gross fraud upon the majority of that congressional district in Arkansas," and the Senator thought that the governor should be prosecuted. Clayton did not let that pass. He observed that the committee report had not used the word "fraud" or made any such allusion. It had simply concluded that Boles was entitled to the seat. Clayton thought it "a strange idea" that issuing a certificate of election in a contested race made the governor guilty of a crime. For three hours Clayton charged Bayard with defending "Ku Klux cut-throats" in the debate over a new Civil Rights bill.[3]

In December of 1872 Clayton debated his Arkansas colleague, Senator Benjamin F. Rice, on whether yet another Congressional committee should investigate affairs in Arkansas. Clayton elicited laughter when he suggested that perhaps Congress should have a permanent committee on Arkansas allegations "to inquire into all the allegations and bring the allegators before them." The committee reported to the Senate on 26 February 1873 that Clayton received a clear majority of both houses of the General Assembly, *not* including those claimed to be fraudulently elected, some of whom voted against Clayton. It noted that Clayton supported

Boles in the election, but accepted the verdict of the Arkansas Supreme Court and the state legislature in granting the certificate. The majority report concluded that the charges against Powell Clayton were not sustained and the Senate accepted the resolution by a vote of thirty-three to six.[4]

What had begun as a political embarrassment to Clayton ended as a political windfall. In his efforts to persuade President Ulysses Grant to remove from office his political enemies, William G. Whipple, United States District Attorney, and Robert F. Catterson, United States Marshal, Clayton was bitterly opposed by his colleague, Senator Benjamin Rice. What was at stake was control of the Arkansas Republican State Committee and with it control of all federal patronage in Arkansas. Senator Rice was unable to persuade Grant to reinstate Whipple and Catterson. Grant instead followed Clayton's recommendations in appointing replacements. However, when the President sent his nominations to the Senate for confirmation, the Senate supported Rice and held up their confirmation.

The power struggle shifted to Arkansas where Rice and Clayton sought to outmaneuver one another in the Republican State Central Committee, but Clayton won the chairmanship of the committee. When Rice led a delegation to the Liberal Republican National Convention in 1872 and supported Horace Greeley for President instead of Grant, the regular national Republican organization backed Clayton. Rice lost his position as Republican National Committeeman from Arkansas and was replaced by Clayton, who then enjoyed the support of the national Republican administration and Republican Senators. As Clayton expressed it, he became "the referee for Arkansas for all federal appointments in every department of the government."[5]

When Senator Rice's term expired 4 March 1873, Stephen W. Dorsey, president of the Arkansas Central Railroad, replaced him. Originally from Vermont, Dorsey moved to Arkansas from Ohio shortly after the war. Despite their control of the regular Republican machinery, the two senators could not prevent the factionalization of Arkansas Republicans. The regular Republicans became known as "Minstrels" and the opposing "reform" or "liberal" Republicans were called "Brindletails." This intra-party division eventually gave Arkansas Democrats the opportunity to regain political dominance in state politics.

Democrats voted with regular Republicans in the election of 1872 to elect Judge Elisha Baxter, a Clayton appointee. A former slaveholder, Baxter had moved to Arkansas from North Carolina in the early 1850s and had been a Unionist during the war. His opponent was Joseph Brooks, the former Iowa chaplain of a black regiment. Black-bearded, heavy-set, and "sullen-looking," Brooks led the Brindletails with a "huge, bellowing voice" and an awesome fury for his opponents. Senator Clayton campaigned in the election, addressing Minstrel Republican gatherings for Baxter. He was frequently heckled, but typically responded forcefully, warning hecklers, "Gentlemen, this is our meeting, and you must behave yourselves. If you do not want to hear me, go out. But we will have order, or we will find a way to secure it. . . ."[6]

State election officials declared Baxter the winner, but Brooks claimed fraud and appealed to the legislature, as provided in the Constitution of 1868. The Arkansas House of Representatives seemed disinclined to investigate, especially since the majority of the committee involved held seats contested by Brooks's supporters. The chairman of the Arkansas Senate Election Committee was Senator John M. Clayton, brother of United States Senator Powell Clayton. In the end, the legislature certified Baxter's election. Governor Baxter, however, alienated many of the regular Republicans who had helped put him in office, including Powell Clayton, and gained support from Democrats by appointing members of both parties to office. He publicly supported an amendment to the constitution which would end disfranchisement in Arkansas. He also opposed legislation for further state aid to railroads.

Meanwhile the Brooks faction assembled evidence of fraud and appealed to the people of Arkansas through the pages of the *Gazette* and other Arkansas newspapers. The Brindles calculated election returns of 43,802 for Brooks and 41,394 for Baxter. Brooks believed that the federal government should intervene because of its constitutional responsibility to assure the states a republican form of government and filed a suit in Federal District Court on 8 January 1873. He was refused a hearing for "lack of jurisdiction."

On 3 March 1873 in an election with a surprisingly small turnout, Arkansas voters accepted the Franchise Amendment, which removed voting restrictions from former Confederate soldiers. The way thus opened for the Democratic Party to gain control of the legislature in the fall election of 1873. Democratic strategy was a cautious policy of maintaining good relations with Republican Governor Baxter.

Legal and political maneuvers to oust Governor Baxter continued for another year, culminating finally in Brooks securing a decision from Judge John Whytock of the Pulaski County Circuit Court recognizing Brooks as governor. Chief Justice John McClure refused to wait for a demurrer to be filed by Governor Baxter and instead secretly(!) administered the oath of office to Brooks. Brooks, taking with him a dozen or so armed men, in effect staged a coup d'etat on 15 April 1874 and literally ousted Governor Baxter from his executive office in the state house. Brooks's men erected barricades on the grounds of the state house and Governor Baxter began assembling troops three blocks east at the Anthony House. Fortunately, United States troops positioned along Main Street separated the two hostile militia to prevent armed conflict. President Grant intervened and ordered Brooks to retire with his forces from the state house and to turn the building over to Secretary of State Johnson. The Arkansas legislature then recognized Baxter as Governor and President Grant ordered Brooks to disperse his forces, which he did.[7]

Governor Baxter eventually filled key offices with Democrats: the Chief Justice, two Associate Justices, the Attorney General, and the Treasurer. The entire episode, known as the Brooks-Baxter War, revealed a shift in strategy by Clayton and regular Republicans in order to prevent the Democratic Party from regaining control of the Arkansas government. Though originally backing Baxter in 1872, Clayton in 1874 supported Brooks and sought to block the adoption of the new constitution.

Although Brooks failed in his bid to wrest the governorship from Baxter, Senator Clayton initiated the resolution in the United States Senate which created the Poland Committee to inquire into affairs in Arkansas. That committee conducted hearings twice in Washington and twice in Little Rock. The Committee ultimately concluded that it was improper for the federal government to interfere with the existing government in Arkansas. After prolonged debate on 2 March 1875 the Senate accepted the report by a 150-81 vote, although Republicans still held a two-thirds majority. In Arkansas "thousands of tongues made the air resound with shouts of rejoicing," wrote the *Gazette*, and Governor Augustus Garland proclaimed "a day of thanksgiving and prayer for the deliverance of the state from her long and dreary condition of bondage."[8]

After again unsuccessfully seeking intervention by a sympathetic but cautious President Grant, Senator Clayton finally capitulated. Clayton advised his followers:

> The action of Congress on Arkansas affairs is conclusive. The validity of the new constitution and the government established thereunder ought no longer to be questioned. It is the duty of Republicans to accept the verdict and render the same acquiescence which we would have demanded had the case been reversed.

Clayton did, of course, blame Baxter for the Republican loss of power in Arkansas. In 1914 he wrote:

> ... from the moment Elisha Baxter surrendered the State Government to the Democrats that party became and has remained supreme in the state.[9]

Meanwhile Senator Clayton was more vocal on the floor of the Senate and had become better known and respected among his colleagues. He served on several committees and was chairman of two. Clayton kept pressure on the Senate to get bills on the floor he was interested in. He showed a dogged persistence, for example, in getting a construction bill passed for a bridge across the Arkansas River at Little Rock. He entered actively into the debate on many issues and was often involved in minutiae and petty questions. He introduced a resolution calling for a National Railroad System, and in the many debates involving railroad construction and operation, Clayton leaned towards a laissez-faire philosophy. In a speech in 1874 Clayton expressed his belief that railroad construction companies should operate with "the least obstacle" from the government. He did, however, believe that stockholders were not sufficiently protected and foresaw a future day when the "great question" of "the abuses of corporations" would have to be faced. He proposed a rather novel idea that stockholders should be made personally liable for the debts of a corporation in which they owned stock up to an amount equivalent to that of the stock they owned. In other words, stockholders could lose the amount actually invested and their share of the debt proportionate to the value of that stock.

Generally Clayton opposed the spending of public funds for private relief. For example, the Senator spoke against paying $5,000 in damages to a White River, Arkansas, cotton planter caught between federal and Confederate lines during the war. The man knew the risks, said Clayton, and "his profits would have been enormous. . . . I have serious doubts as to whether the government should pay at all for damages of this character. . . ." Similarly, he protested using tax money for a Boston relief bill after a disastrous fire. Clayton thought that people whose property was flooded by the Mississippi River would then also have to be indemnified.[10]

Senator Clayton's most spirited, indeed his most eloquent, speeches involved the protection of the civil and political rights of blacks in the South. He voted for a strong civil rights bill to prohibit public segregation and frequently spoke out strongly, even bitterly, against both the Ku Klux Klan and the white "Redeemer" governments which gained control of several southern states while he was a Senator. A sharp exchange between Clayton and Senator Augustus S. Merrimon of North Carolina in December of 1874 illustrated the point. Merrimon delivered a lengthy and indignant protest that any substantial number of whites in the South entertained any ideas of depriving blacks of the franchise. The many civil disturbances in the South since the Civil War, he contended, resulted from blacks being "misled and deceived by wicked and irresponsible men." He wanted the national administration to leave the South alone to manage its own affairs.

The Senator from North Carolina referred to Arkansas as a state where "misrule and usurpation" had produced "almost general anarchy." Nevertheless, the white men of Arkansas had just recently granted full voting privileges to blacks in the Arkansas Constitution of 1874. Merrimon observed that blacks were an essential part of the population: "they are essential as laborers; they are essential as domestics. . . ." The Senator from Arkansas could stand it no longer and asked, "Will the Senator allow me to interrupt him?" A bitter exchange followed. At one point Merrimon told the Senate that it was really the Confederacy that brought freedom to slaves because the Confederacy started the war and the war resulted in emancipation![11]

On 16 January 1875 Clayton finally had the opportunity to speak in detail concerning the "southern question." In a lengthy speech he demonstrated his reputation for being a forceful and eloquent speaker. He also demonstrated a strong dislike for southern Democrats and bitterness that blacks were denied the franchise. Clayton suggested a way to find peace and quiet in the South:

> Let the republican party of the South disband its organization and surrender unconditionally into the hands of the democracy the exercise of all political power; let the republican leaders . . . get beyond Mason and Dixon's line . . . or put padlocks upon their mouths . . . let colored citizens of the South remain in the fields and workshop upon election day and leave our democratic friends the privilege of representing him; . . . let none but white men sit in the jury-boxes, and none but white children have the advantage of the public schools. . . .

Then, Clayton suggested, there would be peace in the South, the kind of peace that exists when a burglar puts a pistol to someone's head and tells him to remain perfectly quiet:

> In that case there would be no noise, no confusion; the neighbors would not be disturbed, no one would be hurt, perhaps, though a little transfer of property might take place.

Clayton charged the Democratic party with "disorder, intolerance, and violence." He referred to many specific disorders existing in the South long before Congressional Reconstruction began. The Ku Klux Klan organization also antedated "carpetbag government." Clayton claimed that the Klan had as many as thirty thousand members in Arkansas as early as the fall of 1868 before there were any charges of increased state debt and when no carpetbagger had yet been accused of "malfeasance or misfeasance in office," and when there were only a total of six blacks in the Arkansas legislature. Clayton further claimed that at that moment the new Democratically controlled Arkansas state militia was composed largely of former Klansmen. The debate waxed increasingly bitter in sarcastic exchanges between Clayton and several other southern Senators, prompting the presiding officer to intervene.

Clayton charged that whites, particularly white law officers, murdered blacks with impunity throughout the South, but when a black murdered a white, the story was played up in the national press and the black was dealt with harshly "under Judge Lynch's authority." Clayton's sweeping indictment of the Democratic Party clearly showed why he was hated so virulently by so many members of that party—the innocent perhaps more than the guilty.

> Are we to look for peace from the party which resorts to murder and violence to obtain possession of political power? I think not. Are we to turn over to their Ku Klux Klan, their White Leagues, and their State militia the colored people of this country?

The South could not be "let alone," as southern Senators expressed it. "I say that a democratic ruffian in the South that has once dipped his hands in the blood of a colored man can never be broken of that habit unless his neck is broken. . . ." "The slave power," Clayton insisted, was not dead but was in the process of regaining most of its lost ground in the South.[12] The consistency and forcefulness with which Clayton pushed for elemental protection of the civil and political rights of blacks indicated his sincerity. He probably hurt himself more politically by not quietly looking the other way as many of his colleagues did. No doubt he often was carried away by his own rhetoric, but he also often referred to specific historical incidents. The success of White Supremacy did, however, also mean the defeat of the Republican party in the South. Republican senators in caucus discussed the problem at length during the month of December 1874. Senator Clayton asked for support in persuading Congress to recognize the Arkansas Constitution of 1868 under which Arkansas was readmitted to representation in Congress and to nullify the Constitution of 1874, but he got little support. Some southern Republican senators advocated the sending of troops back into the South, fearing that the Republican party was "hopelessly dead unless decisive steps were taken during the present session to put down turbulent whites." Several northern senators openly expressed themselves against "further interference with the affairs of the South," saying that they had lost many votes in the North because of it. In the end Congress left the South alone, particularly after the election of 1876.

The Constitutional dilemma was not solved by Reconstruction but in the end simply ignored. Perhaps many considered it unsolvable. "If the Federal Government," asked Congressman Benjamin F. Butler, "cannot pass laws to protect the rights, liberty, and lives of citizens of the United States in the States, why were guarantees of those fundamental rights put in the Constitution at all?" But a law is effective only if it is enforced or voluntarily obeyed. The clear consensus throughout the South was that blacks were not to have equal political rights with whites, at least not in that generation. James Madison had sought to solve the problem in the Constitution, but had been only partially successful. How does a system of government, he asked, protect the minority from the tyranny of the majority? From the Southern perspective the perceived tyranny of the minority Republican governments in the South and the dominance of the federal government over the states gave them the excuse or rationalization to deprive blacks of their civil and political rights. "It remains to be seen," a contemporary observer commented, "how long a minority, however loyal, can govern in a republican country." As long as there was to be majority rule, the Powell Claytons of the South simply could not survive politically at the state level. His influence was national in orientation and dependent upon his control of federal patronage in Arkansas.[13]

As his single term neared its conclusion, Senator Clayton presided over a half dozen meetings of the United States Senate, none of great significance. Capable as he was of pursuing a task energetically and effectively, it was ironic that potentially the most significant position Clayton held while senator was Chairman of the Senate Committee on Civil Service and Retrenchment. "Spoilsman" that he was, one certainly would not expect much reform from him. Indeed, his method of "civil service reform" was a proposal to divide patronage positions according to population among the states! The effect would have been to give the southern and western states more influence within the bureaucracy. Clayton calculated that Arkansas should have 135 employees in the bureaucracy in Washington, D. C., instead of the sixteen that were actually working there at the time. The New York *Times* pointed out that under Senator Clayton's proposal, the 25,000 Republicans in Arkansas would get more offices than the 60,000 Republicans in Kansas. Other senators objected that some of their constituents would lose their jobs and the proposal was voted down.[14]

Clayton often spoke for the Committee on Military Affairs on the floor and frequently sought help for veterans. For example, he worked to give disabled veterans preference in hiring for government jobs. Most of the bills Clayton introduced were "private bills" for the "relief" of one individual or another. Some refined existing laws. Many dealt with Arkansas or the Indian Territory or with railroads. Humor occasionally enlivened routine business. In a discussion of an appropriations bill, Clayton observed that travel in Arkansas was very expensive, and a voice interjected, "and somewhat dangerous!" The motion carried.

Senator Clayton sat through the entire impeachment trial of William Belknap, Secretary of War, without comment and he did not vote on the verdict (which was acquittal). He was not involved, either, in the Electoral Commission debate over the disputed Presidential election of 1876.

Clayton's term as senator ended on 4 March 1877. He was succeeded by Governor Augustus Garland, elected without opposition by a Democratic Arkansas legislature. Clayton had begun his senatorial career under the shadow of innuendoes, allegations, and a pending court case. He ended it as a nationally-known Republican leader, influential both in Washington and among regular Republicans in Arkansas. A front-page editorial in the New York *Times* admitted an earlier prejudice against Clayton and other Southern Republicans. The journalist had initially considered Clayton "a political adventurer of unsurpassable shrewdness, pluck, and unscrupulousness," but concluded that Clayton and others with him had entered politics in self-defense to protect their right to remain in the state unmolested. It was apparent to him that there were "two sides to this Southern question, even in Arkansas."[15]

Notes

[1]*Arkansas Gazette*, March 18-19, 1871.

[2]*Washington Chronicle*, December 21, 1871. United States, *Congressional Globe*, 42d Cong., 2d Sess., Dec. 21, 1871, XLV, pt. 1, 262-63, 311-14. XLV, pt. 2, Feb 9, 1872, 934-38. Appendix, 37.

[3]*Ibid.*, 3706, May 21, 1872.

[4]*Congressional Globe*, 42d Cong., 3d Sess., Dec. 20, 1872, XLVI, pt. 1, 321. United States, *Congressional Record*, 43d Cong., Special Session, March 25, 1873, I, 184-85.

[5]Powell Clayton, *The Aftermath of the Civil War in Arkansas* (New York: Neale Publishing, 1915), 345.

[6]*Arkansas Gazette*, September 29, 1872. John Gould Fletcher, *Arkansas* (Chapel Hill: U of North Carolina P, 1947), 229.

[7]George H. Thompson, *Arkansas and Reconstruction: The Influence of Geography, Economics, and Personality* (Port Washington, New York: Kennikat P, 1976), 97-101. Earl F. Woodward, "The Brooks and Baxter War in Arkansas, 1872-1874," *Arkansas Historical Quarterly*, XXX (1971), 315-36.

[8]*Congressional Record*, 43d Cong., 1st Sess., May 12, 1874, II, pt. 4, 3806. Clayton, 349. *Arkansas Gazette*, March 3, 9, 1875.

[9]Clayton, 166, 349.

[10]*Congressional Globe*, 42d Cong., 3d Sess., Dec. 13, 1872, XLVI, pt.1. *Congressional Record*, 43d Cong., 1st Sess., April 13, 1874, II, pt. 4, 3055. May 15, 1874, 3927.

[11]*Congressional Record*, 43d Cong., 2d Sess., Dec. 22, 1874, III, pt. 1, 191-92. *Congressional Globe*, 42d Cong., May 21, 1872, XLV, pt. 5, 3736, 525-31.

[12]*New York Times*, December 9, 22, 1874. *Congressional Record*, 43d Cong., 2d Sess., March 2, 1875, III, 2073.

[13]*Congressional Globe*, 42d Congress, 1st Session, 223. Whitelaw Reid, *After the War.* (Cincinnati, 1866). Quoted in Eric Foner, *Reconstruction: America's Unfinished Revolution, 1863-1877.* (New York: Harper & Row, 1988), 455, 185.

[14]*New York Times*, June 9, 1876. *Congressional Record*, 44th Cong., 1st Sess., June 7, 1876, IV, pt. 4, 3599-3600, 3647-48.

[15]*New York Times*, October 19, 1874.

Chapter Four

MISTER CLAYTON

Rivaling Powell Clayton's interest in politics was his admiration for the business world. Measuring success in monetary as well as political terms, Clayton was both an entrepreneur and a political leader. He often saw life around him in terms of economic opportunities and possessed the initiative to put his money-making ideas into practice. He was often called "A man of vision" by those lauding his financial ventures. What he lacked in capital he made up in persuasiveness. Investors were frequently attracted to Clayton for his shrewdness and managerial skills and often invested heavily in his ventures. He primed the pump with money of his own, but he seldom had an abundance of investment capital. He supplied the ideas, initiative, and personal contacts, and others supplied the cash.

Clayton went to Arkansas without money but got his start by purchasing a few bales of cotton at the right time and made a profit from his Pine Bluff plantation. Then he invested in railroads and finally put most of his energy into developing the resort town of Eureka Springs in northwest Arkansas. There he gained—and spent—a fortune. Clayton loved the genteel and cultured life of the Gilded Age. He cultivated the life and manners of upper class businessmen. He catered to the rich and they accepted his dignity and charm. The Crescent Hotel in Eureka Springs, which he helped build, was an elegant and popular spa, a gathering place for many American Victorians, including such men as James G. Blaine, Republican candidate for President of the United States in 1884.

Shortly after completing his term of office in the United States Senate in 1877, Clayton became interested in the newly incorporated resort town of Eureka Springs. Located in one of the most beautiful scenic areas of the Arkansas Ozark Mountains, its springs were reputed to have unusual medicinal qualities in healing all manner of diseases and sicknesses. Newspaper reports alleged that as many as 15,000 tourists came in a single year to the tiny village sprawling around the springs. Clayton decided to investigate.

What he saw confirmed his earlier appraisal that Arkansas was indeed "a land of opportunities," as later publicity for his railroad claimed. The nearest railroad came to Seligman, Missouri, eighteen miles from Eureka Springs. A short line to Seligman would not require much capital and should pay rapid dividends. More important, if so many people were flocking to Eureka Springs in spite of the difficulties of getting there, how many could be attracted if a railroad took them all the way? How well might a shrewd businessman profit from a hotel or two, or from the purchase of real estate while prices were still low? The new town needed public utilities and streets. Surely a civil engineer with Clayton's qualifications would be in demand. And a street car system would be useful. Eureka Springs offered an ideal opportunity for such an enterprise. The hills were extremely steep and many of the visitors infirm.

Clayton promptly contacted several close friends to share in both the capital investment for his ventures and the potential bonanza they were expected to yield. Three of those friends joined Clayton in organizing the Eureka Springs Improvement Company, the single most significant force in developing Eureka Springs into a thriving, nationally known resort town. The three were Richard C. Kerens and Arthur Hoyt Foote, both of St. Louis, and Logan H. Roots, a Little Rock banker.

During the Civil War Richard Kerens gained experience in transportation management in the Army of the Potomac and in the Army of the Frontier in Arkansas. After the war he started a transportation company and eventually moved to St. Louis as a director of the St. Louis, Iron Mountain, and Southern Railroad. Besides his partnership with Clayton, Kerens was involved in several other railroad enterprises, including the Atchison, Topeka, and Santa Fe. In 1891 President Benjamin Harrison appointed Kerens as one of the three members from the United States on the Continental Railway Commission to aid in railroad development in Latin America. Kerens served ten years on that board and helped in the railroad survey of fifteen Latin American countries.

Kerens was involved in Republican politics in Missouri in much the same manner as Clayton was in Arkansas. He was Republican national committeeman from Missouri from 1884 to 1900 and thus dispensed federal patronage in Missouri as Clayton did in Arkansas. Kerens was a friend of both James G. Blaine and Mark Hanna, national chairman of the Republican party. He was a member of the national executive committee during five presidential campaigns and served as national treasurer of the Republican party for a time. He gave generously to Republican campaign funds, and in 1909 President Taft appointed him as United States Ambassador to Austria-Hungary for four years. A devout Catholic, Kerens built several Catholic chapels and churches, including St. Elizabeth's Chapel in Eureka Springs, near the Crescent Hotel. He died in 1916 at the age of seventy-three.[1]

Clayton's second partner, Logan H. Roots, was president and principal stockholder of the First National Bank of Little Rock. He had been on General William Tecumseh Sherman's staff during the Civil War, then moved from Illinois to Arkansas and served two terms in the United States House of Representatives, from 1868 to 1871. As Congressman, Roots obtained grants for railroad construction in Arkansas. A political ally of Clayton, he filled the position of federal collector of internal revenue in Arkansas and, later, was United States Marshal for the western district of Arkansas. He was interested in railroads and had the reputation of being "always quick to grasp an inviting opportunity to advance his fortune" and "ever ready to aid young or struggling enterprises that promised prosperity." As head of one of the important sources of investment capital in the state, Logan Roots was exactly the type of person whose friendship Clayton sought to cultivate.[2]

The fourth officer of the Eureka Springs Improvement Company was Arthur Hoyt Foote, a railroad man from St. Louis. Foote served as secretary of the Improvement Company, as manager of the Crescent Hotel, and as auditor, passenger agent, and secretary of the Eureka Springs Railroad Company.[3]

When Clayton, Kerens, Foote, and Roots organized the Eureka Springs Improvement Company in 1884, the resort town was already a bustling village with fifty or more boardinghouses and hotels, a bank, thirty grocery stores, a dozen saloons, twenty-two doctors, one undertaker, twelve real estate offices, three newspapers, and various stables, churches, and bathhouses. One of those early hotels was the "Clayton House," Powell Clayton's first experience in the hotel business.[4]

The stagecoach from Seligman took four hours on a winding dirt road and a ferry crossing of the White River to reach Eureka Springs. Nevertheless, hundreds of people made that

The Clayton House
in Eureka Springs

trip each vacation season. The most immediate opportunity then seemed to Clayton to be a short railroad connection to Seligman. He organized the Eureka Springs Railway Company and sold bonds and common stock at one hundred dollars per share. The company gave one thousand shares of stock to the connecting line at Seligman, the St. Louis and San Francisco Railroad (known as the Frisco Line), which agreed that its rolling stock could be used on the Eureka Springs system.

It would pay the Eureka Springs Railway Company ten percent of its gross receipts from interchange passenger fares and freight. The principal common stockholders were:[5]

Richard Kerens	1,593	shares
Frisco Railroad	1,000	shares
Logan H. Roots	683	shares
Powell Clayton	569	shares

Clayton was the vice-president and general manager of the line. His civil engineering experience enabled him to oversee the construction project and two experienced engineers supervised the actual work. The terrain was exceptionally difficult.

The track descended from 1,540' at Seligman to the White River, back up to 1,143' at Eureka Springs. The grade was as much as 2.6% and the right-of-way twisted serpentinely, following the terrain. There was only one straight stretch of a mile in the eighteen miles of track. Much of the rolling stock used on the railroad was owned by the Frisco Line, but the Eureka Springs company bought a heavy wood-burning freight locomotive named the *Eureka Springs* and a passenger locomotive christened the *Powell Clayton*. Running time from Seligman was one hour for $1.75. Pullman palace sleeping cars ran twice daily from St. Louis to Eureka Springs.[6]

The first year of the Eureka Springs Railway, 1883, was a success. It carried 23,000 passengers and 22,000 tons of freight for a total revenue of $88,247 with overhead of $22,284. Fifty-five thousand dollars went towards funding the initial debt, leaving $10,963 additional profit. Since the $1,500,000 in stocks and bonds represented an actual cash outlay of less than $700,000, the investors' cash investment returned about ten per cent the first year, as well as salaries for the directors.[7]

Clayton's next project was the formation of the Eureka Springs Improvement Company with himself as president and Kerens and Roots serving on the board of directors. The company quarried limestone near Eureka Springs and used it to build the Crescent Hotel, the Presbyterian

Church, the railroad depot, the Palace Bath House, the Basin Park Hotel, and other Eureka Springs buildings. Clayton shipped limestone via his railroad to many places in the midwest. He obtained government contracts to provide stone for public buildings in St. Louis, Kansas City, Springfield, Missouri, and in Harrison and Fort Smith, Arkansas. The Improvement Company purchased several hundred acres of land within the corporate limits of the city and secured a franchise from the city under the name of the Interstate Gas Company to lay gas mains through Eureka Springs. The company charged consumers three dollars per thousand cubic feet of gas and Eureka Springs was soon known for its "splendid gas-lighted streets."[8]

The most spectacular achievement of the Eureka Springs Improvement Company was the Crescent Hotel. The grand opening on 20 May 1886 included fireworks, gun salutes, a parade and band concert, and a ball in the Grand Ballroom of the Crescent, celebrated by over four hundred people. The speaker for the dedication ceremony was James G. Blaine, introduced by Powell Clayton, of course.

Built from local limestone, the Crescent Hotel towered above Eureka Springs from a steep wooded mountainside. Built in American Gothic style, its one hundred rooms accommodated 250 guests and provided a large, elegantly furnished suite for Clayton's family. The hotel was lighted with gas and furnished with electric bells; it was heated with steam and had a hydraulic elevator. Many rooms even had private baths with water pumped from one of the springs. The spacious lobby included a massive fireplace and a promenade deck overlooked the town and gardens. The Crescent dining room specialized in Southern cuisine and mint juleps. Scenic tours were available in carriages. Evenings in the Grand Ballroom women wore the latest Victorian fashions of black velvet and diamonds, brown silk and brocaded satin, or white lace over white silk dresses. Built at a cost of $294,000, the Crescent never was a money-making enterprise in itself. It did, however, attract many visitors who in turn spent money on other, more profitable businesses.[9]

One problem with the picturesque location of the hotel was the difficulty of getting from the railroad station up the extremely steep and winding road of West Mountain. The Improvement Company sent carriages and tally-hoes, a type of coach drawn by four horses in which thirty-five persons could ride, to meet incoming trains. In 1891 a mule-drawn streetcar system was completed. With only three miles of track, the streetcar had to climb 140 feet to the Crescent Hotel. The system was electrified in 1899 by the Eureka Springs Electric and Street Railway Company, another subsidiary of the Improvement Company. With a seating capacity of seventy-five, streetcars ran from early in the morning until late at night for years and became one of the attractions of the city.[10]

Not all of Clayton's efforts went into money-making enterprises. In 1890 the Eureka Springs city council appointed a Board of Commissioners to develop a city water system. The Board elected Clayton as president, who completed the project efficiently. The city council in 1892 created a Board of Public Affairs, composed of private citizens with the responsibility for planning city improvements. That board chose Clayton as chairman and work soon began grading and widening streets and building retaining walls and board sidewalks. During the summer a mule-drawn tank of water sprinkled the streets daily to keep down the dust.[11]

It was characteristic of Powell Clayton's career that where he went, political controversy and confrontation followed. Eureka Springs was no exception. Not everyone was willing to accept his aggressive methods of entrepreneurship. He did, indeed, have a way of getting things done, but he often stirred up hostility in the process. Some cooperated with him; others did not. For the first six years after incorporation many citizens of Eureka Springs bought land without clear legal title. Many claims

Crescent Hotel, Eureka Springs, 1990. The people in the photograph are the author's wife and granddaughter, Wendy.

conflicted, and the Improvement Company developed a compromise settlement which was approved by the voters of Eureka Springs and ratified by a United States District Court on 6 April 1885. Deeds were issued to leaseholders who lived

Interior of Crescent Hotel

on disputed land. Churches received lots without compensation. All spring lands belonged to the city, and all property unclaimed within a specified time would become the property of Eureka Springs Improvement Company. The settlement granted the Improvement Company the right to operate streetcar lines and gas and water lines for fifty years.[12]

Obviously not everyone was satisfied with that arrangement and some thought that the Improvement Company was too powerful. Two principal political factions emerged, identified geographically. "Silk Stockings" lived on Spring Street and West Mountain, and the "Mohawks" were Main Street business owners and residents of East Mountain. The Silk Stockings favored Clayton and/or his interests and the Mohawks opposed him. Two old friends of Clayton assumed the leadership of both factions. Major J. W. True acted as a sort of "ward boss" of the Silk Stockings, and the spokesman for the Mohawks was J. W. Newport.

The Eureka Springs *Daily Times Echo* of 30 July 1891 printed the constitution of the Royal Order of Mohawks, who declared war on "rings, monopolies, trusts and 'bossism'" at the local level. Mohawks were against certain "corporations" in Eureka Springs which had "obtained control . . . of the land and homes of the people—without fee or reward." The Mohawks accused "corrupt influences" of getting thousands of dollars of "the people's money" to use for the building of a railroad. Unidentified persons working under the direction of Clayton allegedly removed landmarks, changed the assessors' books, and raised assessments "in dark rooms, hidden from the people."

A dramatic confrontation between the two factions occurred when the Mohawks sought to prevent the widening and improvement of Spring Street. Early one morning Mohawks gathered with "guns, knives, and all manner of implements of warfare." Major True, in his shirt sleeves and unarmed, marched into the midst of the crowd. Grabbing his pick and turning his back, he began to work, saying, "Now, men, I am unarmed. . . . Assassinate me if you wish." At just that moment Clayton rode down the mountainside with rifle and pistol. He shouted at the group gathered there, "What in the hell does this mean?" and was "unceremoniously" told what it meant by the Mohawks. Somehow Major True persuaded Clayton to leave, since work had already begun. Bloodshed was avoided and street construction continued.[13]

Clayton had ambitions for the Eureka Springs Railway to extend eastward to Harrison and eventually to Helena on the Mississippi River. By merging with the Missouri and North Arkansas Railroad Company in 1906 this was accomplished. The original Eureka Springs Railway Company did reasonably well during its seventeen years of operation, its aggregate operating income of $1,286,415 compared with expenses of $550,308. The original cash outlay returned $692,500 in seventeen years plus salaries for the officers and ownership of St. Louis and North Arkansas securities.[14]

Clayton made a great deal of money; lost a lot on speculative ventures; spent much on a comfortable life style; and gambled away part of what was left. He once lost $25,000 in a single evening of gambling. Often his elegant living quarters were more of a front than a reflection of wealth. His investments and gambling sometimes left him with inadequate funds for his family. A frequent complaint of his wife, Adaline, was that her husband sometimes left her without enough money for normal family expenditures. A letter from the Crescent Hotel, for example, from Mrs. Clayton to her daughter instructed Charlotte to pay express charges on a package she would be receiving, for which her mother would reimburse her later. Mrs. Clayton's explanation was, " . . . I have no money now, and your father has such a poverty-stricken spell on him. . . ." Powell Clayton's will provided for $25,000 for each of his children, but little remained for his wife.[15]

Notes

[1]*The National Cyclopedia of American Biography* (New York: James T. White and Company, 1918), XXXI, 408-409. Allen Johnson and Dumas Malone, *Dictionary of American Biography* (New York: Charles Scribner's Sons, 1930), V, 353-54.

²United States Congress, *Biographical Directory of the American Congress, 1774-1927* (Washington, D.C.: Government Printing Office, 1928). 1633. George H. Thompson, "Asa P. Robinson and the Little Rock and Fort Smith Railroad," *Arkansas Historical Quarterly,* XXXIX (1980), 7. *National Cyclopedia,* V. 95-96.

³June Westphal and Catherine Osterhage, *A Fame Not Easily Forgotten* (Conway, AR, 1970), 38-39.

⁴Cora Pinkly-Call, *Pioneer Tales of Eureka Springs and Carroll County* (Eureka Springs, AR, 1930), 46. The "Clayton House," located at 211 Spring Street in Eureka Springs, is now called "Crescent Cottage" and has been remodeled in typical Victorian style.

⁵James R. Fair, Jr., *The North Arkansas Line: The Story of the Missouri and North Arkansas Railroad* (Berkeley, CA: Howell-North Books, 1969), 2-5.

⁶Fair, *North Arkansas Line,* 5-14. *Arkansas Gazette,* February 3, 1883.

⁷Fair, *North Arkansas Line,* 11-14. Lawrence R. Handley, "A Geography of the Missouri and North Arkansas Railroad," unpublished M. A. thesis, University of Arkansas, 1973.

⁸Westphal, *Fame Not Forgotten,* 42-43. *Arkansas Gazette,* May 22, 1886.

⁹*Daily Times-Echo* (Eureka Springs), May 20, 1886. Westphal, *Fame Not Forgotten,*. 97-100. Fair, *North Arkansas Line,* 14-19.

¹⁰Westphal, *Fame Not Forgotten,* 56-58. Fair, *North Arkansas Line,* 29.

¹¹Westphal, *Fame Not Forgotten,* 49-56. Pinkley-Call, *Pioneer Tales,* 66.

¹²Oklute Braswell, ed., *History of Carroll County, Arkansas* (Berryville, AR: Braswell Printing Co., 1889). Westphal, *Fame Not Forgotten,* 22-26.

¹³*Daily Times-Echo* (Eureka Springs), July 30, 1891. Westphal, *Fame Not Forgotten,* 62-66. Pinkley-Call, *Pioneer Tales,* 66-67.

¹⁴Fair, *North Arkansas Line,* pp. 31-103. Handley, *Geography,* 62-63.

¹⁵Adaline Clayton to Charlotte Clayton, September 17, n.d., Powell Clayton Papers, Special Collections, University of Arkansas, Fayetteville. Personal conversation of the author with Kathleen Moncheur, June, 1980.

Chapter Five

BOSS CLAYTON

By the time United States Senator Powell Clayton completed his term of office, he was recognized as the head of the Arkansas Republican party by the national leadership. He had held two high elective offices and had led the Arkansas delegation to the 1872 Republican National Convention in Philadelphia. His years in Washington provided useful contacts for Arkansas Republicans. With the party permanently out of power at the state level, Clayton sought to establish Republican influence in scattered local enclaves within Arkansas, particularly through the control of federal patronage within the state. Except for the administrations of Grover Cleveland, Republicans held the Presidency from 1868 to 1913 and Clayton, therefore, controlled most federal appointments in Arkansas for half a century. For nearly forty years he was a member of the Republican National Committee.

Since delegate strength at national conventions was based on state population rather than relative party strength, Arkansas took sizeable delegations to those conventions. Clayton was identified with the Stalwart faction of the national party, those who believed in the control of federal patronage by regular state and local party bosses. Half-breed Republicans were willing to approve civil service reform. The 1880 Republican National Convention deadlocked between Stalwarts and Half-breeds in the longest stalemate in Republican history. Neither Stalwart leader Ulysses Grant nor his Half-breed opponent, former Speaker of the House James G. Blaine, could obtain a majority of delegate votes. The convention finally settled for a compromise candidate, James A. Garfield. Not surprisingly, the entire Arkansas delegation of twelve voted for Grant on all thirty-six ballots.[1]

President Garfield won the 1880 election and agreed to "consult" regular Republican organizations before making appointments. He appointed Blaine Secretary of State. In the summer of 1881 a disappointed Stalwart assassinated the President. The new President, Chester A. Arthur, replaced Blaine as Secretary of State.

Alienated Blaine forces prepared for the 1884 Republican National Convention ready to contest an Arthur nomination. In the process of lining up southern delegates for Blaine, his supporters persuaded the Stalwart-dominated Republican National Committee to recommend Powell Clayton as temporary chairman of the convention. Clayton showed his flexibility and political opportunism in switching from Arthur to Blaine. Some of the younger Republicans such as Henry Cabot Lodge, Sr., and Theodore Roosevelt preferred a deadlocked convention, hoping to nominate a reform-minded candidate. For that reason Lodge and Roosevelt challenged Clayton's appointment as temporary chairman, not as an affront to Clayton, but as a test of Blaine's strength. Lodge nominated John R. Lynch, a black Congressman from Mississippi, as chairman instead of Clayton. Independents dominated the ensuing debate and Lynch won the chairmanship, 424 to 384. Clearly, Blaine had to come to terms with the reform element in the party, and Clayton was the loser.[2]

Blaine won the Republican nomination, but lost the Presidency to Democrats for the first time since the Civil War. Significantly, the reform wing of the Republican party, derisively named "Mugwumps," bolted the party and supported Cleveland in the election, giving him just the margin he needed. Lodge and Roosevelt stayed with the Republican party, warning that a party split would cost them the election. It did, and with the election went thousands of patronage positions. Theodore Roosevelt stated the problem for the reformers: " . . . civil service reform is not safer in Mr. Cleveland's hands than in Mr. Blaine's. . . ."[3]

Things looked bleak for Arkansas Republicans, long shut off from state office and then deprived of federal patronage. Clayton, though, was not one to acquiesce without a struggle. His opportunity came with the unwillingness of the Arkansas Democratic leadership to pursue policies demanded by Arkansas farmers. That failure almost cost Democrats the Arkansas election of 1888. Realizing the strength of the Agricultural Wheel and its political ally, the Union Labor Party of Arkansas, Clayton decided to coalesce with discontented Democratic farmers.

The regular Democratic party panicked. The Wheel was by far the most popular farm organization in Arkansas. Democratic papers labeled Wheelers "tools of Republicans." The Cleveland County Democrat claimed that "Boss Clayton" would win a place in Benjamin Harrison's cabinet if he and the Wheel-Republican coalition could carry Arkansas. Clayton unwittingly played into Democratic hands in an August speech at Eureka Springs when he said:

> I am going to vote for Norwood [Wheel candidate for governor.] I do not object to voting for a Confederate soldier [who] when he found he was in error, acknowledged the wrong and came over to the Republican side.

Democrats capitalized on Clayton's political *faux pas* and the *Gazette* warned that Arkansas had only two choices in the election: "the Democracy" or "Republicanism." The race issue was also exploited: a vote for the Wheelers was a vote for Negro Republicans.[4]

Election Day, 3 September 1888, saw the largest gubernatorial voter turnout in Arkansas history. Democrat James Eagle received 99,214 votes to C. M. Norwood's 84,213. The losers claimed fraud, but Governor Eagle held his office. The Republican-controlled United States House of Representatives conducted hearings and unseated the Democratic Congressman from the First District. In the Second Congressional District, Wheelers had supported Powell Clayton's brother, John M. Clayton, against United States Representative Clifton R. Breckinridge. Election officials declared Breckinridge the winner by a vote of 17,857 to 17,001. John Clayton contested the outcome and on 29 January 1889, while seeking evidence in Plummerville to support his case, he was murdered—shot at close range through a window. The House investigated and nearly two years later ruled that the election was fraudulent. Breckinridge, however, immediately regained his seat in the 1890 election two months later.[5]

Powell Clayton was one of the nine members of the National Committee in charge of preparations for the 1888 National Convention, and he and Logan Roots led the Arkansas delegation of fourteen. Benjamin Harrison of Indiana was nominated and with the Mugwumps back, Republicans narrowly won in New York and in Indiana and took the election, 233 to 168 electoral votes.[6]

President Harrison's election stimulated patronage squabbles among Arkansas Republicans and many chafed under Clayton's dominance. Two unsuccessful efforts were made at state conventions to defeat Clayton and the state chairman of the party, Henry Cooper. By that time Harmon L. Remmel, a Little Rock businessman, was a member of the state executive committee and Clayton's trusted ally. Clayton had some difficulty getting all his appointments through the Harrison patronage system and wrote the President that a "wrong" appointment would "very much embarrass" him in his efforts to "serve" Harrison in Arkansas.[7] Pushing for the replacement of a Democratic appointee in the Hot Springs post office, Clayton wrote the President, "It is hard to build up a party in the South" without patronage. Clayton opposed the appointment to federal office of William G. Whipple, mayor of Little Rock, citing a lack of party loyalty and party work as his reason. Whipple, Clayton's long-time political enemy, had supported the Greeley Movement in 1872 and had not contributed financially to the organization. In February 1892 Clayton warned President

Harrison that there were in Arkansas "some disappointed and disgruntled" Republicans who would like to "make war" on the re-nomination of Harrison at the state convention. Clayton hoped that the Republican opposition never would be able to claim that Democrats had had greater influence with the President in an appointment than the Republicans. Clayton thought that Blaine should not have "interfered" in an Arkansas post office appointment. Clayton wrote "plainly" to Harrison, he said, because Harrison's "interest" was more at stake than his. He simply wanted to do his "duty" to Arkansas Republicans who were depending on him "to represent their interests."

The President must have mollified Clayton because Harrison wrote to Clayton a few months later after the 1892 national convention expressing gratitude to Clayton for his role in securing his renomination. Harrison wrote that he "never had a doubt that the part of the line you commanded could not be driven back an inch. . . ." However, Harrison lost the 1892 election and Grover Cleveland returned to the White House. The Democratic party, for the first time since before the Civil War, controlled both houses of Congress, the Presidency, and federal patronage.[8]

Four years later the stage was set for the most significant Presidential election in decades. Republicans were anxious to return to power; Democrats were determined to stay there; and militant Populists charged that neither party sought to meet the growing problems of the American farmer and the new industrialism. Mark Hanna, the National Chairman of the Republican party and campaign manager for Ohio Governor William McKinley, sought the support of regular Republicans in Southern delegations to offset opposition from Eastern Republicans. Clayton, as a member of the National Committee and boss of one of the Southern state organizations, was important to Hanna's strategy. Thirty-five of the fifty members of the National Committee agreed to "stand firm for the right," which meant approval of McKinley delegates from the Southern states. Clayton voted with the thirty-five and brought a unanimously pro-McKinley Arkansas delegation to the convention. In each case of contested delegates the National Committee seated only McKinley delegates. McKinley won easily on the first ballot.

Republican campaign headquarters for 1896 was in Chicago, since the Upper Middle West was the most competitive region. Clayton was a member of the executive committee in the New York campaign office and scheduled most speaking engagements during the campaign in the East and South. Democrats and Populists both nominated the eloquent Nebraska Congressman William Jennings Bryan, but in a very close race

McKinley won the Presidency.[9]

Whatever the Republican victory of 1896 meant to the nation ideologically, it also meant that many federal offices would be occupied by Republicans instead of by Democrats. Powell Clayton was not first in line for patronage, but he had a lifetime of political indebtedness in his favor for his faithful and productive service to the Republican party and had played an important role in the campaign. Clayton never had sought appointive office for himself but now considered the time right to do so. McKinley considered him for a cabinet-level position, but Clayton preferred being Minister to Mexico, a rather quiet, pleasant post among the cultured Mexican aristocracy. The position paid $17,500 a year plus a $5,000 contingency fund and allowed enough leisure time to permit continued involvement in Arkansas Republican politics through his longtime friend and political assistant, Harmon L. Remmel.[10]

As one would expect, many members of the Republican State Central Committee of Arkansas, including several federal office-holders, heartily recommended Clayton for the position he sought, citing his "earnest labor . . . to advance [Republican] principles" in the South. One suggested that Clayton was "beloved and admired by all men who [were] not blinded by partisan prejudices." More accurately, a St. Louis friend reminded McKinley that Clayton had been "of inestimable service to your friends when true allegiance was very necessary."[11]

Not everyone was so enthusiastic, of course. "An insult to Mexico," protested the New York *Times*. Clayton knew nothing about Mexican culture or the Spanish language. He was "conspicuously unfit" for any important position. The *Times* lamented that "the appointment was the payment of a political debt. In fact were it not for the "enlightened character" of Mexican President/Dictator Porfirio Diaz, the United States might be in for serious difficulties.[12]

The *Arkansas Gazette* was more philosophical, though probably no happier, about Clayton's appointment. The Republicans had won the election, so why begrudge them the spoils of office? A front-page cartoon depicted little pigs going to market with the caption: "Little Republican Office-Seeking Pigs." The next day Clayton appeared with a crown on his head as the king dishing out "official pie." Clearly Clayton got his slice. The *Arkansas Democrat* thought that "the one armed Arkansan" would "out-rank all southern Republicans" for a cabinet position; it was time for General Clayton "to come into his reward." The *Democrat* believed that such a high office would be "of incalculable benefit to the South"—presumably by getting Clayton out of the state.[13]

On 25 March 1897 the State Department officially notified Clayton of his appointment as Envoy Extraordinary and Minister Plenipotentiary of the United States to Mexico. The Department issued Clayton a special passport for himself and suite and a letter of credence addressed to the President of Mexico. Clayton relinquished management of the Eureka Springs Railway and leased the Crescent Hotel for a five-year period. He departed for Mexico City, accompanied by his wife and daughter Charlotte. Another daughter, Lucy, was married, and his youngest, Kathleen, was in boarding school near Philadelphia. Lieutenant Powell Clayton, Jr., was stationed at Fort Leavenworth, Kansas, with the Fifth Cavalry.[14]

From Mexico City, Clayton attempted to retain his control of Arkansas Republican politics through his spokesman and principal informant, Harmon Remmel. Remmel served one term in the Arkansas House of Representatives, was permanent chairman of the 1890 state convention, and a delegate to the 1892 and 1896 national conventions. In 1895 he was elected president of the Arkansas League of Republican Clubs. It was obvious from the uncharacteristic candor with which Clayton wrote many letters to Remmel from Mexico City that the latter was a close confidant of the ambassador.[15]

Clayton had maintained solidarity within the state executive committee in order to ward off challenges to the established leadership from the outside, but within the ruling oligarchy, power struggles sometimes occurred. Dissidents sought to exploit both Henry Cooper's and Harmon Remmel's interest in the position of United States Marshal for the Eastern District of Arkansas. The two key leaders avoided an open split by a compromise whereby Cooper was appointed marshal and Remmel collector of internal revenue. Since Cooper's position paid $1,000 a year more than Remmel's, Cooper agreed to pay Remmel $500 a year to "equalize" the two salaries. Clayton did not approve the arrangement but did nothing to prevent or change it. He agreed that Remmel would be next in line for the marshal's job but was concerned to find a position for Harry F. Auten, a newcomer from Michigan, whose loyalty he sought to secure with a proper "reward for his services." Clayton instructed Remmel to hold the state convention early in June 1898 and to nominate Auten for governor, as long as he would endorse the national platform adopted at St. Louis. Auten was nominated but made a very poor showing, receiving only 27,000 votes out of 100,000.[16]

In October 1898 Cooper suffered a stroke and was near death for several months. Remmel, though next in line for Cooper's job, wanted to keep his position as collector and still name Cooper's successor so he could continue collecting his $500 a year kickback, so he wrote Clayton for permission to succeed Cooper as chairman of the state central committee so that he would be the "proper person to be recognized by the President . . . when it comes to appointments." A week later Remmel wrote again that he had just about reached an agreement with Auten for marshal. With Auten's forces and the group at Fort Smith, together with Remmel's at Little Rock, they "would virtually have matters in their own hands" throughout the state and Clayton would then know definitely that he had a "lieutenancy" that could "positively be relied upon."[17]

However, with Clayton out of the country and preoccupied with his new job, Auten decided to challenge the regular Republican machine rather than to cooperate with it and began to organize support against the Clayton-Cooper-Remmel triumvirate. Clayton warned Remmel not to announce for the chairmanship but simply to work on lining up "the friends who stood together in the past." Publicly, Remmel was to work against the "kickers" by letting it be known that whatever the convention decided about the chairmanship would be satisfactory to him. Privately, he would do everything he could to get pro-Remmel delegates elected to the convention. Clayton wrote to many other "friends" and instructed them to keep silent on the chairmanship issue. First win control of the convention; then the choice of chairman was no problem. Remmel, of course, had competition for the chairmanship position. Judge Jacob Trieber was a possible contender. Remmel accompanied him on a trip to Washington to sound him out. Trieber told Remmel that he did not want the chairmanship because it cost too much money and took too much time. Asbury Fowler of Little Rock was interested and was maneuvering for support in the Pulaski County central committee and in Texarkana.[18]

In a stormy session at the state convention Clayton and Remmel managed to defeat the opposition. Strangely enough, their chief support came from Fowler and his Pulaski County organization. Auten's bid for power came through his efforts to get more black delegates elected to the national convention. He was aided in this by Scipio A. Jones, secretary of the Pulaski county central committee and one of the leading blacks in Arkansas. Since Auten's and Jones's splinter group was unable to secure recognition from the state convention, Clayton and Remmel remained in control. The regular Republicans from Pulaski county condemned Auten and Jones for "stirring up race hatreds." Fowler's help in Pulaski county was crucial, motivated probably by his "lily-white" beliefs. In gratitude and as a show of unity, Remmel later resigned from his position on the executive committee of the national Republican League and nominated Fowler as his replacement. One of the most influential blacks in Arkansas, John E. Bush, remained with the regular organization and criticized blacks who bolted the convention with the white insurgents. Bush was Receiver in the Internal Revenue office at Little Rock and remained in that position until 1913, when Democrats returned to the Presidency.[19]

So the old guard maintained control and the 1900 state convention re-elected Clayton as Republican national committeeman from Arkansas and chose him as president of the convention and Jacob Trieber as first vice-president. The convention selected the fifty-seven members of the state central committee, including Clayton, Cooper, and Remmel. A convention resolution pointed "with pride to the highly successful career" of their "distinguished leader, General Powell Clayton as ambassador to Mexico," and expressed appreciation that the Republican party of Arkansas "enjoyed the privilege of his wise counsel." Clayton told the convention that it was his "painful duty" to announce the resignation of Cooper. Immediately after the convention adjourned, the state central committee convened and elected Remmel chairman and Trieber, vice-chairman.

Since Auten had broken with the regular Republicans, the state convention nominated Remmel for governor. That seemed to be more than a gesture on the part of Arkansas Republicans; Remmel was an effective campaigner and a friend of many conservative Democratic businessmen. But he was no match for Democrat Jeff Davis, one of the most colorful demagogues in Arkansas history. Davis identified Remmel as the tool through whom the New York insurance trust was prepared to seize control of Arkansas. Remmel, Davis charged, had appointed a "kinky-headed negro" to his staff at the collector's office. And, worst of all, he was Powell Clayton's servant who was trying to re-establish Reconstruction rule in Arkansas. Remmel lost in his bid for governor by a vote of 88,000 to 40,000.[20]

Ambassador Clayton took one of his frequent leaves of absence in June 1900 to attend the Republican national committee meeting in Philadelphia and the Republican National Convention. For the first time since 1868 Clayton was not a delegate to the convention. President McKinley informed the various state Republican parties that he did not want any federal office-holder whom he had appointed to be a delegate to the convention. The President sought to avoid any appearance of a conflict of interest whereby people under obligation to him would feel constrained to re-nominate him. He also wanted to demonstrate to the American voters that he had enough support within the party without the top level state Republican leadership participating in the convention.

Consequently, neither Clayton nor Remmel was part of the Arkansas delegation of sixteen, as they normally would have been. Neither was Harry F. Auten. Charles D. Greaves, later a major participant in the 1902 insurgent movement in Arkansas, was a member of the delegation. Usually J. E. Bush would have been one of the few black members, but his federal office prevented his selection. The state convention chose another black, Fred Havis, instead. McKinley had appointed Havis postmaster at Pine Bluff, but, because of the strong opposition of Arkansas Democratic Senator James H. Berry, the United States Senate refused to confirm his appointment. Scipio Jones's participation in the Auten revolt did not prevent him from being a delegate to the national convention. Clayton told a reporter from the St. Louis *Globe-Democrat* that he "fully concurred" in the principle that it would not be "the part of good taste" for federal office holders to be delegates to the national convention.[21]

The Republican National Convention met in Philadelphia in June 1900 and, of course, re-nominated President McKinley. Since Vice-President Garret Hobart had recently died, competition focused on the vice-presidency. Mark Hanna's opponents sought to reduce his influence in the party by nominating the Governor of New York, Theodore Roosevelt. The leverage they used to secure southern votes for Roosevelt was the re-opening of the "southern question." Since delegate strength at Republican national conventions was based on state population rather than on numerical party strength within the state, southern party bosses, such as Clayton, had a disproportionate influence in national politics compared to party leaders in strongly Republican states. Senator Matthew Quay, Republican boss of Pennsylvania, proposed electing four delegates at large from each state with one additional delegate for each 10,000 Republican votes in the preceding election.

Obviously this alarmed Clayton and other southern Republican leaders. With little voice in state politics, they would lose some of their national influence. Blacks, especially, stood to lose. Effectively disfranchised in the South, they still had a minor political role in the Republican party and in the distribution of Republican patronage. For a decade Hanna had cultivated support among southern blacks, often paying their expenses to national conventions. If southern Republicans lost representation nationally, so also would Hanna. McKinley stood to lose, too: in the 1896 convention 289 of 317 southern delegates had voted for him, but only 347 of 554 northern delegates.[22]

Clayton was in a dilemma. He opposed Roosevelt's blustering, direct manner and disagreed with some of his policy positions, and he remembered Roosevelt's opposition to his nomination as temporary chairman of the 1884 national convention. But Clayton's biggest problem with Roosevelt's candidacy was the fact that restive Arkansas Republicans were already moving towards the Roosevelt banner in an effort to break the Clayton-Remmel-Cooper hold on the regular Arkansas Republican party. Southern delegates to the national convention met at the headquarters of the Arkansas delegation on the night of 20 June to plan their strategy for the floor fight which they anticipated would occur the next day. John McClure of Arkansas was elected chairman of that meeting of southern delegates who then chose a steering committee to represent them. Powell Clayton, who was not a delegate to the convention, was elected chairman of the steering committee. Remmel and other southern delegates visited several northern delegations, trying to persuade them to vote against the adoption of Quay's resolution. Nevertheless, Quay's tactic worked: McKinley pressured Hanna to accept Roosevelt, and in exchange for Quay's withdrawal of his resolution, southern delegations fell in line and, in the interests of "party unity," nominated Theodore Roosevelt for Vice-President of the United States.

Republicans of Arkansas worked for President McKinley's re-election in 1900 and succeeded in reducing the Democratic majority in Arkansas from 72,591 in 1896 to 36,342. Mark Hanna urged Remmel to run for governor because it could influence the national race, since Arkansas voted in September, earlier than most of the rest of the nation. (Running for governor also strengthened Remmel's position in the regular party machine.)[23]

Clayton returned to Mexico after the national convention, declining an invitation to participate in the speaking campaign in Ohio. He contributed $300 to the Ohio state central committee and more to the national fund. Soon he began preparing for the next convention. He wrote to Remmel in August 1901 to "try to ascertain if there [was] any Roosevelt movement in Arkansas." The Clayton-Remmel team were to "work with the original McKinley men in the next convention." To be sure that the "friends of President McKinley" were in a position to affect the course of events, he instructed Remmel to communicate with Hanna regarding the appointment of a bank examiner at Fayetteville and the postmaster at Huntsville. He warned Remmel of a fellow-Republican whose loyalty he suspected because he had written to Clayton, "Hurrah for Theodore Roosevelt for the next President." Clayton expected Hanna to be the next President and worked to keep Arkansas's eighteen delegates pro-Hanna. In return he expected cooperation from Hanna and

McKinley for the Clayton-Remmel machine. Always alert to "plots" against him or "disloyalty" to regular Republicans, Clayton warned Remmel of attempts to organize young Republicans in Arkansas, "a mischievous movement, fraught with much danger." He suggested that Remmel try to infiltrate the new organization:

> If you had some young men whom you could trust, and who have not been too prominent heretofore, in some of the back counties, whom you could get to write carefully prepared letters to [Sid B. Redding, president of the state Republican League] asking his advice as to the desirability and manner of organizing young Republicans, you might obtain valuable information.[24]

The assassination of President McKinley in the summer of 1901 came as a shock to Ambassador Clayton. He immediately submitted his resignation to the new President, but Roosevelt, desiring to keep the regular Republican organization intact, informed Clayton that he wanted him to continue in the office which he had filled "so satisfactorily." Clayton was grateful. He wrote Roosevelt that he knew he had "no claim whatever" upon him, but now was "indebted" to him. He promised Roosevelt actions that would aid in making Roosevelt's administration a success just as he had for McKinley.[25]

President Roosevelt continued to allow Clayton and Remmel to control federal patronage in Arkansas, but insurgents hoping to secure Roosevelt's recognition of them as the Roosevelt faction, openly attacked the Clayton-Remmel machine. Clayton and the state central committee responded by freezing insurgents out of federal patronage whenever possible. Ben Foreman of Texarkana complained that all his supporters were turned down for federal office. Clayton defended himself: after Foreman's "declaration of war upon me and my friends he cannot expect any favors . . . to help him fight his battles against the organization of the party and against me personally." To Remmel he confided that if Foreman and other political enemies had their way, "they would have retired us both from politics."[26]

The Democratic state central committee saw this Republican intraparty strife as a contest between the "Pie Eaters" and the "Pie Hunters" because the distribution of federal patronage was a major issue in dispute. But disagreements went beyond patronage squabbles. The issue was the type of political structure Arkansas Republicans would have: a tightly controlled machine or one with broader, more democratic political participation. Insurgents began to organize. The chairman of the Miller County Republican central committee wrote to the Secretary of the Interior that if a Republican opposed Clayton, he was denounced as a "disorganizer . . . no matter how much he might have done for the party."[27]

Shortly after President McKinley's death, Remmel met with President Roosevelt to learn his attitude toward the previously pro-McKinley-Hanna regular Republican organization. He reported a "pleasant and satisfactory" interview with the President to the *Gazette*, which reported that

> some people . . . predict that the new President will not be guided and bound by the voice of the Republican state central committee when it comes to distribution of federal offices in Arkansas.

The regulars passed their first test of influence with Roosevelt in December 1901 when the President followed all the recommendations of the state central committee for postmaster appointments. In March 1902 Roosevelt told Fowler he would recognize the regular organization as long as it recommended, "good, clean men."[28]

That same month H. F. Auten went to Washington to prefer charges of misconduct against Remmel and others on the state central committee. President Roosevelt instructed the Postmaster General to investigate and Clayton immediately rushed to Washington. The Arkansas Republican state central committee denounced Auten and ousted Foreman from his position on the committee. "We denounce and condemn," the committee declared, "the recent attempt of certain persons assuming to themselves political importance to seriously injure the cause of Republicanism in this state. . . ." The committee reaffirmed its support for Remmel, Roosevelt, and their "great leader, now absent in a foreign country in the discharge of his exalted duties as ambassador."[29]

The *Gazette* interviewed the insurgents. One claimed that the Republican organization in Arkansas had existed for thirty years purely for the distribution of federal patronage. Another claimed that many postmasters were induced to buy policies in Remmel's insurance company. The *Gazette* was gleeful that at last Arkansas Republicans were "unmasking each other." The editorial page carried such comments as, "Republicans are in politics for themselves, Democrats for their country."[30]

Words turned to blows one spring day when Auten went to Remmel's Mutual Life Insurance offices in Little Rock to demand a retraction of an article that Remmel had written for the *State Republican*. Remmel's article stated that Auten opposed Remmel because Remmel opposed Auten's appointment as United States attorney for the western district. The article also claimed that Auten had tried to negotiate a salary-"equalizing" scheme with another political appointee. Auten took a loaded cane with him to Remmel's office and, when Remmel refused to retract his article, struck him with it. Remmel warded off the blow and several assistants came to his aid. Auten explained to the *Gazette* that Remmel

> attempted to make some insulting remarks and I struck him and took him by the throat, but before I could give him the punishment he so richly deserved several of his clerks pulled me off.

Auten further called Remmel a liar, scoundrel, and coward, and charged him with compelling a postmaster at Russellville to hire a particular person as assistant postmaster and divide the postmaster's salary with him. The Pine Bluff postmaster was required to pay $1,000 a year to "one of Remmel's henchmen."[31]

Clayton was in the United States nearly two months; by the time he returned to Mexico he thought he had the political situation under control. He confided to Remmel in April that he believed "Auten and gangs are now completely discredited." Perhaps so, but the opposition had succeeded in persuading President Roosevelt to remove from office the number two man in the regular Republican organization, Harmon L. Remmel himself. The Remmel-Cooper "arrangement" had finally surfaced and Roosevelt fired Remmel as Internal Revenue Collector. Clayton and Remmel tried to discover the leak and traced it to an inadvertent slip from Cooper to Foreman, who had once been greatly admired by Cooper. Auten, too, had known what was going on.[32]

Clayton was scarcely back in Mexico when the Stuttgart *Republican*, encouraged by Auten's success in removing Remmel, called for a rally of insurgents. "Now is the Time for Arkansas Republicans to Break Loose from Claytonism" the headlines read. The insurgents sought to "dethrone Remmel and corporation" and to reform the Republican party of Arkansas. No longer would a policy in Remmel's insurance company be necessary "to secure a post office." According to the Republican newspaper, Remmel had not only "shared" Cooper's salary, but was "a contemptible patronage broker, demanding and receiving cash tribute" from office-holders he had aided. Clayton received his "patronage money" salary and was allegedly busy with "financial schemes in Mexico." The article renamed the state central committee the "Arkansas Tammany." Insurgents demanded reforms placing party matters "directly in the hands of the common working Republicans." No office holders would be permitted on the executive committee. The newspaper called for an "Insurgent Convention." Anticipating a charge of disrupting the party, it claimed to be merely "disrupting the machine." Remaining loyal to the "policies and principles of McKinley and Roosevelt," the *Republican* urged each county to send delegates.[33]

President Roosevelt sent a personal representative to observe the two rival Republican state conventions. The report circulated anonymously that he planned to recognize the faction which made the best showing at the polls. Insurgent Harry Auten organized the first Republican Roosevelt Club in Arkansas in 1902, significantly at Eureka Springs, Clayton's home. Regular Republicans denounced the insurgents and issued a four-page flyer with the headline, "The Republican Organizations of Arkansas Stand Together as a Unit" and in caps: "ALL LOYAL TO REMMEL!" The state central committee resolved to stand united, "as strong and impregnable as Gibraltar."[34]

Three hundred insurgent delegates from all over the state met in Little Rock on 26 June 1902 and nominated Charles Greaves of Hot Springs for governor and called for a Republican organization "controlled by the people and not by a boss." Greaves charged that the Republican party of Arkansas was dominated by a "junto." Loyalty meant "absolute lack of individuality." Office-holders "were willing to divide salaries, pay tribute, lend servile homage and eat all sorts of political locusts and wild onions to retain themselves in office." Greaves called for reform so that no member of an Arkansas Republican state or county committee could hold federal office. The insurgents elected a state committee composed of ninety-five members, one from each county, and twenty at large, chosen by the convention. Greaves was cheered when he told the assembly that "no ambassador of the United States" presided over that convention. Ben Foreman of Texarkana asked, "Who turned Arkansas over to the Democrats?" "Clayton! Clayton!" shouted dozens of voices. Insurgents lampooned the Clayton-Remmel alliance and the regular Republicans' "spontaneous tribute to Marsa Powell" which praised the "wisdom and ability" of chairman Remmel: "Wisdom, because he too is supposed to be the only one who knows just what the general knows in far off Mexico. . . . Ability, because he can draw the salary of two offices and not fill either one. . . ."[35]

The regular Republicans in their June meeting elected Remmel chairman of the state committee, in spite of his removal from federal office. Clayton explained to Roosevelt:

> The high esteem in which he is held and his previous unsullied record caused the Republicans of the state to believe that he had been sufficiently punished

for his indiscretion by the loss of his office and the humiliation resulting therefrom. . . .

Clayton pledged to Roosevelt the support of the Arkansas delegation in 1904—insofar as he was "able." Clayton charged Democrats with putting Republican insurgents on county election boards instead of regular Republicans and inquired of President Roosevelt his response to claims by Greaves and the insurgents that Roosevelt had promised to recognize their recommendations to federal office in Arkansas if they developed a larger vote in the 1902 state elections than the regular Republican organization.[36]

President Roosevelt reassured Clayton. He had, at least after the September election, decided to stick with the regulars. Roosevelt wrote in October 1902:

> The result in Arkansas was to my mind absolutely conclusive in showing that the voters were with the regular organization. How I wish we could get a Republican Congressman from Arkansas![37]

The year 1903 was quiet for Clayton in Arkansas and in Mexico. He was on leave during April and May and spent much time in Cuernavaca, Mexico. In June he sailed on a voyage to New York and then to Belgium to accompany home his daughter, Baroness Charlotte Moncheur. Roosevelt wrote Clayton in July:

> I hope you can attend in person the meeting of the National Committee next January. Then I should like to have a full talk with you over the whole situation.[38]

By 1904 with an eye as always toward the elections of that year, Clayton had shifted his ideas on patronage so that they more nearly approximated those of President Roosevelt (and those of the more moderate Republican insurgents). The *State Republican* reported that General Clayton had written a "strong letter" to the Republican state committee for a "just and fair distribution of federal offices" in Arkansas. The most "healthy party growth" would result if federal offices were rotated with two terms being the normal tenure. The ambassador, too, thought the selection process should be more democratic in order to avoid "unseemly squabbles for office." A federal office was not the "personal property" of the office-holder and must be shared with other "deserving" Republicans.[39]

Clayton cautioned President Roosevelt, however, about restrictions on the political activities of federal office-holders. He agreed, no doubt reluctantly, that no office-holder should go as a delegate to the national convention, but public officials should be able to participate in political activities without neglecting their duties. To prohibit such activities, Clayton believed, was "an infringement upon their rights as citizens." Clayton warned Roosevelt that he had found in Arkansas "quite a strong Hanna undercurrent," but the Arkansas state central committee passed Clayton's resolution endorsing the Roosevelt candidacy. Sounding like a Populist himself, Clayton wrote Roosevelt that if he were not nominated, "it would be the result of the secret machinations of the great moneyed combinations known as trusts." Secretary of the Interior Ethan Allen Hitchcock was trying to keep federal land officers in Arkansas from party activity and Clayton could not afford to lose the cooperation and services of those influential men in the event of a Theodore Roosevelt-Mark Hanna contest. Significantly, Clayton added almost as an afterthought, "Remmel . . . will work faithfully for you."[40]

In April Clayton requested a fifty-five day leave to attend both the Arkansas state convention and the Republican national convention. He believed he could put together a delegation "absolutely loyal" to Roosevelt, of "true and active Republicans," made up largely of businessmen who were not interested in office but in the "triumph of Republican principles." "What I want," Clayton wrote,

> is to secure a state and district delegation upon whom we can absolutely rely in all contingencies. . . . The party in Arkansas is in excellent condition. Two of the counties where insurgents were strongest during the last election, have held their conventions, the insurgents coming back into the organization and participating, receiving of course a hearty welcome. The ringleaders still hold out, but are being deserted by their following. . . .[41]

Hanna died of typhoid fever on 15 February 1904, and Roosevelt entered the national convention without effective opposition. In the general election the Roosevelt-Clayton-Remmel team further reduced the Democratic plurality in Arkansas, to 17,700 votes. The regular Republicans were elated. In a "Monster Meeting of Arkansas Republicans," Remmel read a telegram from their "grand old man": "In spirit I am with you all tonight. Let unity and circumspection be our watchword."[42]

Clayton announced his intention to resign as ambassador on 4 March 1905, Roosevelt's inaugural day. Remmel applied for the position of United States Marshal of the eastern district, received the endorsement of the state committee, and in due time, Roosevelt appointed him to that office. Greaves, Auten, and Foreman became largely ineffectual in Washington.

An editorial in the *State Republican* explained why:

> The President exercises his own judgment, but whenever an organization is known to be effective and representative, he relies very largely on its advice in making appointments to office.[43]

By the time of Roosevelt's southern tour in 1905 Clayton was solidly part of the Roosevelt team. He had proved a loyal supporter of the President and was amply rewarded with patronage and influence in Washington. Clayton was no longer ambassador to Mexico by that time and was on the Reception Committee to welcome the President to his seven-hour visit to Little Rock on 25 October 1905. Enormous crowds greeted Roosevelt and perhaps as many as 40,000 people heard his speech at Glenwood Park. Clayton accompanied the President throughout the day and was one of the seven honored guests to be seated at the Presidential table at the luncheon given in Roosevelt's honor. Clayton "held frequent conferences" with Roosevelt during the day, and a spirit of camaraderie was evident between the two men. Clearly Powell Clayton and the regular Republicans had the ear of the national administration.[44]

Boss Clayton was a successful politician. He set out to control Arkansas Republican politics and federal patronage in Arkansas and did so. He was astute and aggressive, the counselor of Presidents, senators, congressmen, judges, and national party leaders. As the acknowledged leader of the Arkansas wing of the party, he acted as a member of the Republican general staff. As such, he considered his political opponents the "enemy" and sought to defeat or isolate them. They responded in kind. Commander Clayton expected, and usually received, support from the lesser party leadership, often from sentimental sycophants. It was incumbent on minor functionaries of the party to give ungrudging support to the top leadership. In exchange, they received promotions within the party and federal patronage.

Unlike most politicians Clayton looked upon compromise as a weakness. He preferred to manipulate rather than to compromise, to "punish" his "enemies" rather than to conciliate his opponents. Consequently, he generated both loyalty and animosity wherever he went. Authoritarian both in philosophy and personality, he did indeed deserve the title "Boss Clayton."

Notes

[1]Republican Party, *Official Proceedings of the Seventh National Convention*, Chicago, 1880. Francis Curtis, *The Republican Party: A History of Its Fifty Years' Existence and Record of Its Measures and Leaders, 1854-1904* (New York: G. P. Putnam's Sons, 1904), II, 65-90.

[2]Curtis, *Republican Party*, II, 116ff. John Roy Lynch, *The Autobiography of John Roy Lynch: Reminiscences of an Active Life* (Chicago: U of Chicago P, 1970).

[3]Republican Party, *Official Proceedings of the Eighth National Convention*, Chicago, 1884. Curtis, *Republican Party*, II, 137. Theodore Roosevelt to R. R. Bowker, October 31, 1884, Curtis, *Republican Party*, II, 157.

[4]Clifton Paisley, "The Political Wheelers and Arkansas' Election of 1888," *Arkansas Historical Quarterly*, XXV (1966), 16. F. Clark Elkins, "The Agricultural Wheel in Arkansas, 1882-1890," unpublished D.S. dissertation, Syracuse U, 1953.

[5]United States House of Representatives, *Clayton vs. Breckinridge*. 51st Cong., 1st Sess., 1890. Report #2912.

[6]Republican Party, *Offical Proceedings of the Ninth National Convention*, Chicago, 1888. Congressional Quarterly, *Guide to U.S. Elections* (Washington, D. C.: Congressional Quarterly, 1975), 31-35.

[7]Henry Cooper to Joab Copeland, November 21, 1891. Henry Cooper to Jacob Treiber, March 27, 1892. Henry Cooper to D. B. Russell, December 17, 1891. Henry Cooper to I. Glaspy, November 27, 1891. Harmon L. Remmel Papers, Special Collections, University of Arkansas, Fayetteville. Powell Clayton to Benjamin Harrison, August 20, 1889. Clayton to Harrison, March 20, 1890. Clayton to Harrison, February 15, 19, 1892. Harrison to Clayton, June 13, 1892. Benjamin Harrison Papers.

[8]Benjamin Harrison to Powell Clayton, June 13, 1892, Benjamin Harrison Papers.

[9]Stanley L. Jones, *The Presidential Election of 1896* (Madison: U of Wisconsin P, 1964), *passim*. Theodore Roosevelt, *Selections from the Correspondence of Theodore Roosevelt and Henry Cabot Lodge, 1884-1918* (New York: Charles Scribner's Sons, 1925), 236. Arthur Wallace Dunn, *From Harrison to Harding: A Personal Narrative* (New York: G. P. Putnam's Sons, 1922), *passim*.

[10]Powell Clayton to Harmon L. Remmel, January 2, 1897, Harmon L. Remmel Papers, Special Collections, University of Arkansas, Fayetteville.

[11]Department of State, Appointment Papers, National Archives, Record Group 59.

[12]*New York Times*, February 5, 1897; March 19, 1897; April 25, 26, 1897.

[13]*Arkansas Gazette*, March 14, 1897; March 16, 17, 1897; March 19, 1897. *Arkansas Democrat*, November 17,1896.

[14]*Arkansas Gazette*, March 19, 1897.

[15]Clayton to Remmel, May 18, 1897, Remmel Papers. Marvin F. Russell, "The Rise of A Republican Leader: Harmon L. Remmel," *Arkansas Historical Quarterly*, XXXVI (1977), 234-57.

[16]Clayton to Remmel, October 25, 1897, March 28, 1898, Remmel Papers.

[17]Remmel to Clayton, October 27, 31, 1898, Remmel Papers.

[18]Remmel to Clayton, October 18, 1899, Remmel Papers.

[19]Richard L. Niswonger, "Arkansas Democratic Politics, 1896-1920," unpublished Ph.D. dissertation, U of Texas, 1973, 255.

[20]Russell, "Republican Leader," 245-50.

[21]*Arkansas Gazette*, February 22, 24, 27, 28, March 22, June 19, 1900.

[22]*Southern Representation in the Republican National Convention*, pamphlet in the Pratt Remmel Papers, Special Collections, University of Arkansas, Fayetteville. Marion G. Merrill, *The Republican Command, 1897-1913* (Lexington, Kentucky: UP of Kentucky, 1971), *passim*.

[23]*Arkansas Gazette*, June 21, 1900. Mark Hanna to Richard A. McCurdy, June 21, 1900, Harmon Remmel Papers.

[24]Clayton to Remmel, September 12, 18, 1900; June 21, August 20, 1901, Harmon Remmel Papers.

[25]Alvey Adee to Clayton, September 30, 1901, *Despatches from United States Minister to Mexico, 1823-1906*, Department of State, Washington, D. C., Record Group 59, M97, volume 152. Clayton to Roosevelt, October 10, 1901, Theodore Roosevelt Papers.

[26]Clayton to Remmel, November 11, 1901, Harmon Remmel Papers.

[27]Thomas Orr to Ethan Allen Hitchcock, December 17, 1901, Harmon Remmel Papers.

[28]*Arkansas Gazette*, November 2, December 10, 1901, January 30, March 5, 6, 1902.

[29]*Arkansas Gazette*, March 7, 1902.

[30]*Arkansas Gazette*, March 7, 8, 11, 1902.

[31]*Arkansas Gazette*, March 20, 1902.

[32]Clayton to Remmel, February 2, 1902, April, 1902, Harmon Remmel Papers.

[33]*Stuttgart Republican*, June 12, 1902, Pratt Remmel Papers, Special Collections, University of Arkansas, Fayetteville.

[34]*Arkansas Gazette*, June 20-26, 1902. Four-page flyer, n.d., Pratt Remmel Papers.

[35]*Stuttgart Republican*, June 12, 1902, Pratt Remmel Papers.

[36]Clayton to Roosevelt, September 27, 1902, Roosevelt Papers.

[37]Roosevelt to Clayton, October 4, 1902, Roosevelt Papers.

[38]Roosevelt to Clayton, July 20, 1903, Roosevelt Papers.

[39]*State Republican*, January 6, 1904.

[40]Clayton to Roosevelt, January 15, 1904, Roosevelt Papers.

[41]Clayton to Roosevelt, April 2, 1904, Roosevelt Papers.

[42]*State Republican*, December 2, 1904.

[43]*State Republican*, January 26, 1906.

[44]*Arkansas Gazette*, October 26, 1905. Cf. Willard B. Gatewood, Jr., "Theodore Roosevelt and Arkansas, 1901-1912," *Arkansas Historical Quarterly*, XXXII (1973), 1-24.

Chapter Six

AMBASSADOR CLAYTON

In Mexico City Clayton received a warm welcome, especially from the American colony. The *Two Republics* found Clayton "commanding of appearance," "eloquent," and "polished." General Clayton, wrote the Mexican *Herald*, would make a "diplomatically correct" representative of the United States. He was "correct" when he formally presented his credentials to President Porfirio Diaz, assuring the Mexican ruler that his Excellency's name was "distinguished throughout the United States" for the stability of his government. Official Mexican-American relations in 1897 were excellent and Clayton intended to keep them that way.[1]

Diaz's orientation towards the United States was explicit in his reply to Clayton at his formal reception: Diaz claimed that "the Mexican people" had taken the United States as a "model for their political institutions" and were imitating their northern neighbor in the "intelligent development of their natural resources." Ignacio Mariscal, Mexican Minister of Foreign Affairs, referred to the "noble attitude" of the American people in helping to obtain the withdrawal of the French from Mexico in 1867. The mood of the Mexican government called for restraint, dignity, and courtesy on the part of the American minister. General Clayton fitted the picture admirably. He respected the authority of the Mexican government and realized the limitations of his own position. He was a businessman and welcomed the Mexican government's encouragement of American and European investment capital.[2]

Clayton began his diplomatic duties efficiently. He was assisted in the work of the legation by three male secretaries and military attaché Lieutenant Powell Clayton, Jr. The new minister's initial inventory of his office in the legation told of a drab and uninspiring place to work. A photograph of Clayton working in his office made the point more forcefully. His furnishings included a painting of George Washington, two cuspidors, two oil stoves, and a dilapidated typewriter in need of replacement. The level of activity was perhaps suggested by the need for two cuspidors but only one wastebasket.

The routine work of the legation included correspondence relating to occasional murders of or by American citizens; requests for extradition;

official statistics and lists of publications regularly sent to the State Department; disputes over the amount of customs duties charged Americans; an agreement on regulations to prevent collisions at sea; permission for various scientific groups to enter Mexico. Plans called for the convening of an International Sanitary Conference, an International Library Congress, and a Good Roads Congress. The University of Pennsylvania conferred on President Diaz an LL.D. degree, likening him to "builders" such as Washington, Lincoln, and Juarez. American ranchers whose cattle strayed south of the Rio Grande had to obtain permission from the Mexican Foreign Office to enter Mexico in search of them.[3]

Clayton disposed of all these matters methodically. He had the ability to get to the heart of a problem quickly and if a matter attracted his interest, he pursued it with energy and determination and was not one to be put off easily. His ignorance of Spanish did not impair his routine performance as minister, but it limited his insight into contemporary Mexican politics. He associated almost exclusively with the aristocratic Mexicans of Mexico City and Cuernavaca, many of whom spoke English.

During this time the State Department was not yet organized by regions. The small size of the Department enabled the Secretaries and staff to exert a close centralized control of United States legations, embassies, and consulates from Washington. Many State Department "Instructions" revealed a direct oversight of routine matters, particularly when money was involved. For example, Secretary of State John Sherman (or perhaps an aide) wrote Clayton on 27 October 1897: "The feather dusters and desk baskets are not supplied by the Department. They may be purchased from your contingent fund." Later, Secretary of State John Hay responded negatively to Clayton's request for $8.51 for the purchase of a lawnmower. The Department was even reluctant to allow the construction of two sets of book shelves in the Embassy; it agreed to give the matter "consideration" if Clayton would submit a detailed statement and drawing of the dimensions and material needed.[4]

More interesting than most of those other matters was Clayton's role in encouraging neutral cooperation from Mexico and obtaining intelligence during the Spanish-American War. Official Mexico sought to maintain a posture of "strict neutrality" during the conflict between the United States and Spain. In practice, however, Mexico seemed more willing to cooperate with the United States than with Spain. Shortly after the outbreak of hostilities Mexico announced its intention of observing current international law respecting neutrality, stating that Mexico's relations were "equally friendly" with both belligerents.

General Clayton seldom got excited in performing his ministerial duties, if one can judge by his official dispatches. The Spanish-American War, however, affected him differently. He seemed suspicious, aggressive, and sometimes overly dramatic. The State Department provided $1000 for surveillance of Spanish ships and "all suspicious vessels." Clayton's team of two kept watch on the shipment of goods from Vera Cruz and followed the activities of Spanish citizens in Mexico City. The American minister reported to the State Department names, sizes, and speeds of ships, the number of masts, number of guns (dismounted before entering a neutral harbor), passengers who disembarked, and the cargo carried.[5] The Mexican foreign office patiently cooperated with Clayton's petty questions as to the status of certain Spanish merchant ships, and one Spanish captain was fined fifty dollars because his men called the passengers of another ship "Yankee s.o.b." At times Clayton sought to plan naval strategy from his office in Mexico City and some of his suggestions sounded more like instructions. The State Department ignored him. Surprisingly little appeared in his dispatches concerning American ships in Mexican ports where they received regular cooperation and no harassment. Acapulco was particularly strategic because of its excellent harbor and location on the Pacific coast. It was used as a coaling station for American ships making the long voyage from the west coast, around Cape Horn, to the Caribbean. At the end of the war the United States Secretary of the Navy thanked the Mexican government for its courtesy in permitting the at-cost sales of coal and provisions to American warships.[6]

President Diaz reported to the Mexican Congress shortly after the war that "no controversy or difficulty arose with either of the belligerent powers." Mexico soon added the rank of ambassador to her diplomatic corps and both the United States and Mexico on 1 January 1899 promoted their ministers plenipotentiary in Mexico City and Washington, D. C., to ambassador and designated their legations as embassies.[7]

Mexico participated in the First Hague Peace Conference in 1899, and at the request of the United States, the Second International Conference of American States met in Mexico City. Designed to be another small step towards inter-American cooperation, the conference deliberately avoided substantive agreement in order to prevent controversy. Ambassador Clayton arranged for housing for the American delegation but was not involved in the conference and showed no more than perfunctory interest in it. Clayton viewed inter-American conferences with distrust, seeing in them efforts to establish an alliance of Latin American states hostile to the United States.[8]

During President Theodore Roosevelt's administration Clayton's role as ambassador remained essentially the same as it had been under President McKinley. One of his duties was to determine when the Mexican judicial system failed to provide justice for American citizens and thus required diplomatic intervention. Normally an American citizen residing in Mexico immediately found himself in jail as soon as he was implicated in a crime. Because of the cumbersome judicial system, it was often weeks or months before release on bail. On the other hand, Mexicans charged with crimes against Americans, even the crime of murder, often were freed on technicalities. Clayton gradually became aware of that pattern of events and, with the concurrence of the State Department, brought the situation to the attention of the Mexican Foreign Office. Foreign Minister Mariscal promised to investigate but obviously disliked interference with what the Mexican government considered local matters. The Mexican political system was based on a tacit understanding of non-interference in regional or provincial matters by the federal government in exchange for cooperation and subordination by local authorities in national matters.

Several incidents illustrated the types of problems confronting Ambassador Clayton. In March 1904 in Ciudad Porfirio Diaz in northeastern Mexico, a United States Army corporal was murdered by a Mexican, but Mexican authorities released the murderer without a trial. Clayton investigated, but the only testimony he was able to get was that the soldier slipped and struck his head on the sill of a door while he was leaving a bar.[9]

Another American citizen, Michael Green, found himself penniless in Mexico City on 4 June 1897 and asked a passer-by for five cents to secure a night's lodging in a stable. Mexican police arrested him for vagrancy and sent him under military guard to a convict farm in the state of Oaxaca. When Clayton tried to locate him, the Spanish contractor, Candido Fernandez, denied that he was on the farm. Green eventually smuggled out a letter from the camp to Clayton and the Ambassador then had tangible evidence to present to the Mexican foreign office. According to three eye-witnesses, Green was beaten to death on 29 July 1897, and one of the witnesses was tortured to make him retract statements he had made. Mariscal admitted wrongdoing on the part of Fernandez, but it took five years for Fernandez to be tried in the Mexican courts. The trial court eventually sentenced Fernandez to three years imprisonment, but the Superior Court of Oaxaca reversed the judgment of the lower court and released the prisoner. Secretary of State John Hay wrote to Clayton, "There seems to be no escaping the conclusion that there has been a failure of justice in this case." Hay authorized Clayton to request indemnity for Green's heirs; $3,000 seemed "appropriate." Seeking indemnity from the Mexican government was easier than collecting it, however. Mariscal came up with the novel idea that since both the Chief of Police in Mexico City and Fernandez had acted beyond their legal authority, the Mexican government could not be held liable for their extra-legal or illegal acts. The governor of Oaxaca claimed that the rights of aliens under international law only included "cases of notorious injustice, those in which the infraction of the laws is palpable and 'obvious to the world'"[10]

A rather strange case was that of Francisco Savinien, an American newspaper correspondent, charged with defamation of character of President Diaz's wife. He spent six months in jail for writing a newspaper article in the St. Louis *Post Dispatch* wondering why Mrs. Diaz had twice won the grand prize in the national lottery. Clayton thought Savinien "very imprudent" for "dragging her name before the public in this manner." Apparently it did not occur to him to question the authority of the Mexican government over what an American citizen published in an American newspaper.[11]

Even the American embassy did not avoid occasional harassment by Mexican police. On 24 November 1902 Clayton's servant was arrested for leading his two coach horses with halters instead of bridles. The servant informed the police that the horses belonged to the American ambassador, and the President's son, Captain Porfirio Diaz, passing by at the time, gave them the same information. That did not dissuade the police. Scarcely-restrained anger showed in the letter Clayton dashed off to the Foreign Secretary:

> As Your Excellency knows, this is not the first time that I have been compelled to complain of the unwarranted action of the police, and I beg Your Excellency will cause proper instructions to be issued so that such annoyances and irregularities may not occur in the future.

Mariscal probably issued those instructions because Clayton never again complained of similar problems.[12]

Many railroads in Mexico during the Diaz period were built, owned, and operated by Americans, and many of the employees were American citizens. The Mexican legal system provided that whenever anyone was injured on the railroad (and there were many accidents), the engineer and either the brakeman or conductor were automatically arrested, regardless of whether there was any indication of negligence. The railroad officials were eventually freed and occasionally fined if negligence was involved, but in the meantime, they sat in a Mexican jail.

Ambassador Clayton had frequent discussions with Mariscal concerning the matter and eventually corresponded with all the various Mexican railway companies regarding the nationalities of their employees and their involvement in accidents. Clayton compiled statistics showing that Americans had a larger percentage of arrests than other nationalities. He found that out of a total of 4,009 railroad employees in Mexico, 1,123 were Americans. Of 666 engineers, 477 were Americans. Thirty-two Americans and twenty Mexicans had been arrested in connection with railroad accidents the preceding year. Through the persistent efforts of Ambassador Clayton, sweeping policy changes were made by the Mexican government. The Mexican Department of Justice instructed officials not to arrest railroad employees unless the evidence pointed overwhelmingly towards negligence and to grant release on bail as soon as possible. The effect was dramatic. Clayton in a follow-up study found much speedier and more lenient handling of cases. By the end of 1903 the arrest rate was only 3.3% of the total number of employees for Americans, 4.6% for Mexicans, and 6.3% for other nationalities. Many arrested were held only one or two days and then released. Small fines were imposed in cases of negligence.[13]

The early twentieth century was a violent period on the Mexican-American border. One complaint after another demanded "justice" and punishment of criminals. Murder, petty thievery, raids, and harassment by customs guards were commonplace. Mariscal charged that American officials often took away serapes or hats from Mexicans or made them pay customs duties on them. Cattle rustling was common. Groups of Papago and Yaqui Indians often raided and killed. Mexican bandits operated on both sides of the Rio Grande.[14]

Such incidents no doubt seemed far removed from diplomatic maneuvering in Mexico City, which focused, particularly during Roosevelt's administration, upon a Central American canal, either in Nicaragua or Panama. Though the United States ambassador in Mexico City was not a participant in the historic drama taking place in Central America, he did occasionally take an indirect part. For example, towards the end of 1901, the State Department instructed Clayton to contact the Nicaraguan minister in Mexico City and say to him:

> "Question of route is being strongly pressed. It is absolutely necessary for us to know at once whether or not Nicaragua accepts our propositions in case that route is chosen."

A week or so later Clayton received the following telegram in cipher:

> Ask the Nicaraguan minister to cable modifications. You can put them in Embassy cipher. Congress meets in a few days and it is absolutely necessary to know at once whether satisfactory arrangements can be made with Nicaragua.[15]

When Panama, with the aid of the United States Navy, proclaimed its independence from Colombia in November 1903, Mexico was alarmed. Not wanting to confront the foreign minister directly with the matter, Clayton learned through the Cuban minister in Mexico, who had discussed the situation with Mariscal, that Mexico was not at all pleased with the "secession of Panama" and regarded it as a "very dangerous precedent for Mexico."

Mexico opposed an American presence in Central America for fear of being encircled on both southern and northern borders, and because Mexico had long considered Central America within her own sphere of influence. During the Spanish colonial era Central America had been under the Vice-royalty of New Spain (i.e., Mexico) and when Mexico gained its independence from Spain in 1821, Central America joined the first Mexican empire until it became independent in 1823. In 1885 Guatemala, aided by Honduras, sought forcibly to unite Central America. President Diaz, who, according to a Mexican historian, "envisioned himself ruler over the greater Mexican nation extending from the Rio Grande to Panama," threatened war with Guatemala.[16]

Mexico delayed recognition of Panama until 1 March 1904, but finally, in keeping with traditional diplomatic practice, extended *de facto* recognition. President Diaz explained to the Mexican Congress:

> Recent events on the Isthmus of Panama are sufficiently familiar, as are also the circumstances under which that ancient portion of Colombia proclaimed its independence. . . . A great number of European nations and some nations on this continent had from the start extended recognition of the new republic. At length popular suffrage in those regions gave to the new government a status of regularity and on the other hand there is no danger of its being soon or easily overthrown. . . .[17]

Ambassador Clayton's persistence and patience were rewarded in the issue of the Pious Fund claims of the Catholic Church of California against Mexico, so much that an elated Secretary of State wrote Clayton: "The Department congratulates you on your successful conduct of the negotiations in this matter." The Pious Fund was originally set up by the Spanish royal government from private and public donations to provide income for Catholic missionaries to pacify and convert Indians in outlying Spanish-American territories. Interest from that permanent "pious fund" helped to maintain the Jesuit and Franciscan California missions. When Mexico won its independence from Spain in 1821 the Mexican national government administered the fund for the benefit of Catholic missions in Mexican territory, principally in California. Both the fund and the missions prospered for a time, but in 1842 President Antonio Lopez de Santa Ana ordered the properties of the pious fund sold and the proceeds paid into the national treasury. The Catholic Church was to be compensated for its loss from tobacco income, but the Mexican government made no payment to it after 1842. The treaty of Guadalupe Hidalgo in 1848, ending the Mexican War and ceding California to the United States, included the proviso that all debts and claims which citizens of the United States might allege against Mexico were thereby cancelled. The Mexican government then took the position that the debt settlement included the cancellation of the pious fund since the Catholic Church of California was then part of the United States. The Catholic Church disagreed. So did the government of the United States, stating that the treaty did not release Mexico from the claims of its own citizens.

In due time the Court of Arbitration in The Hague decided in favor of the United States and the bishops and instructed Mexico to pay interest and a perpetual annuity. Mexico paid the amount stipulated promptly during Clayton's tenure as ambassador, providing a diplomatic victory for Clayton personally. That was also an important pioneering effort in arbitration in the peaceful settlement of international disputes since the decision of October 1902 was the first decision by the Permanent Court of Arbitration at The Hague.[18]

A treaty signed by Clayton in 1905 placed fifty-eight bancos, small strips of land caused by the eroding and shifting waters of the Rio Grande, under the permanent jurisdiction of Mexican or American sovereignty, regardless of changes in the river. Two exceptions to that arrangement were a large banco near Eagle Pass, Texas and a large tract of Mexican territory south of the river near El Paso called "El Chamizal." Most of that land eventually went to Mexico during President Lyndon Johnson's administration. The principle, however, was permanently established in 1905 to ignore shifting boundary lines unless they involved tracts of land of more than 625 acres or a population greater than two hundred.[19]

Ambassador Clayton often walked something of a tightrope, caught within the tensions and competing interests of his day. He saw his role as a spokesman for the interests of his government and his country and, to a lesser degree, sought to aid private American citizens residing in Mexico. He was clearly aware of the importance of doing what he could to please key American politicians, but he was just as conscious of the limitations of the pressures and sanctions available to an ambassador residing in an authoritarian state. Disposed to be authoritarian and legalistic himself, Clayton often seemed to empathize more with the top officials of the Mexican government who treated him so courteously and who so obviously wanted good relations with the United States, than with those fellow-countrymen, some of them in Mexican jails, who found themselves caught in the maze of the complex, and seemingly arbitrary, Mexican legal system. Clayton was often reluctant to exert pressure on the Mexican government, increasingly aware of how tenaciously it could refuse to act when it did not want to.

In one series of claims it took almost the entire length of Clayton's term, from 1897 until January 1905, to obtain decisions in favor of American creditors. The court record numbered 22,000 pages and claimants were paid sums totaling hundreds of thousands of dollars. In replying to Hay's letter of congratulation to him for his successful efforts on behalf of American creditors, Ambassador Clayton made the revealing comment:

> American creditors have President Diaz to thank, as it was not until I personally brought the matter to his attention and obtained his assurances that the litigation would be expedited, that any substantial headway was made towards settlement.[20]

Of all the sensational Mexican court cases from 1897-1905 involving Americans in a murder, charges of false imprisonment, or disputes over property ownership, none received so much notoriety as the Mealy case. Newspapers throughout the United States picked it up as a good news item. The United States Senate discussed it, and senators from both sides of the aisle demanded a State Department investigation into Ambassador Clayton's handling of the case. The Secretary of State took a personal interest and informed the President of the case. Clayton traveled to Washington to discuss the Mealy case. American citizens living in Monterrey circulated a petition for the ambassador's removal, and Clayton's enemies, searching for scandal to use against him, discovered his ownership of certain shares of stock in a mining company not involved in the Mealy case.

William H. Mealy moved to Mexico in the 1880s to capitalize on the generous mining concessions available from the Diaz regime. Staking claims near Monterrey and Saltillo, he eventually developed properties valued at more than two million dollars. A dispute over ownership of one of the mines involved him with local Mexican politicians, with relatives of the Minister of War, the Minister of Justice, and even with a son of President Diaz. Unperturbed, Mealy kept pressing his claims until he ended up in a Monterrey jail. His demands to the ambassador to go see the President or to "do something" became increasingly insistent as Clayton was unable to accomplish much on his behalf. American newspapers began publicizing the story and interest grew throughout the country. Mealy instructed his attorneys to prepare a detailed statement of the case and sent copies of it to American newspapers, English-language newspapers in Mexico City, and to the State Department. Clayton referred to Mealy's pamphlet as a "scandalous document." Clayton accused Mealy of lying to the court, of exaggerating his description of jail conditions, and of using consular envelopes to mail his pamphlets. Clayton had been "positively assured" by Mariscal that all of the proceedings in the Mealy case were "perfectly regular and in strict compliance with Mexican law."[21]

In the meantime Mealy's attorneys presented a derisive defense before the appellate court in Mexico City. Mealy was accused of "most tremendous but imaginary crimes. . . ." The charge of theft of civil court records was "a judicial phantom"; indeed, the judge himself was guilty of "an aberration scarcely conceivable in a public functionary." In due time the *New York Times* and other American newspapers reported that the Supreme Court of Appeals of Mexico had exonerated Mealy, that he was not guilty of contempt of court or of perjury, and that the imprisonment of Mealy by the District Court of Ciudad Porfirio Diaz was "irregular and arbitrary." Unfortunately that was not true. Perhaps the *Times* hastily read too much into the court decision. The appeals court did revoke the arrest order and refunded the bond posted, but it was careful to justify the judge in practically every action; there was "data sufficient to proceed against the accused" and the arrest order was not wrongly issued. The court did, however, hold that Mealy's actions were "at bottom, exculpations" and "in consideration of human equity and liberty" the charges were revoked.[22]

So Mealy won his case, regained his liberty, and held onto his property. If Clayton considered that an exoneration of his policy of leaving the matter largely with the courts, his enemies (including Mealy by that time) believed the results were in spite of Ambassador Clayton rather than because of him. Mealy did not give any credit to Clayton, and others informed American newspapers that Clayton owned stock in a rival company to Mealy's. (One Associated Press dispatch "alleged" that he held 100,000 shares.) Later reports made it plural: "companies." Certain unnamed Mexican government officials were also "interested" in the same company. A United States senator suggested the "impropriety of a minister being a member of a large mining company which is looking for favors from the Mexican government," and sought to prevent diplomatic officials "from engaging in speculative mining enterprises." An editorial entitled "Powell Clayton as a Miner" appeared in the *Arkansas Gazette*. The editorial admitted that Clayton had never engaged in any private enterprises that were not legitimate while he was involved in Arkansas politics; he had never invested in mining and had kept himself free from all scandals. In fact, Clayton "knew how to distinguish his politics from a hole in the ground. . . ." However, he was now charged with digging for gold in Mexico and of "being interested" in a certain mining company. The charges sounded ominous since the story came "from the Mexican capital" and was "in the form of an affidavit written in Spanish."[23]

Clayton's explanation soon made it clear that the one company that he had "connections" with, the tiny El Carmen Mining Company, had nothing to do with any of Mealy's companies. His one hundred shares of stock had a face value of $445 and a current market value of twenty-five cents a share. Clayton claimed he had acquired the stock in order to qualify as one of the directors of the company so that he could look after the interests of an aging widow who was his relative. He felt a special obligation toward her because her husband had bequeathed him $20,000. El Carmen had "no litigation of any kind, nor . . . favor to ask of the Mexican Government, . . . no conflict with Mealy," and no Mexican official was a stockholder. Furthermore, it never paid its stockholders a dividend. The State Department accepted the ambassador's explanation and so reported to the press. Because of the publicity given his El Carmen stock Clayton notified the president of the company that he wanted to resign as director when his term expired in February 1904 and to transfer the stock he held back to its original owner. He wrote the State Department that his action was "not prompted by any sense of impropriety" in his holding the stock in trust.[24]

Ambassador Powell Clayton often attracted criticism, much of which stemmed from differing perspectives and expectations of his role as American ambassador. Clayton was always conscious of the primary reason he was in Mexico City: to communicate the official position of his government to the Mexican government. He regarded diplomatic intervention always as secondary to his main task, and he realized the limitations of what he actually could ask or demand from the Mexican government. Judging from the large number of letters in the embassy files, private American citizens seemed to assume that all they needed to obtain "justice" (usually interpreted as a dispute decided in their favor), was for the ambassador to contact President Diaz about the problem. When he refused to do that, Clayton was often accused of not wanting to do his "duty" or siding with the Mexicans in the dispute. Many thought that an American ambassador should "get tough" in defending the national honor and not "tolerate" insults against the flag of the United States, even when neither honor nor insults were at issue. Many American residents of Mexico assumed that they should have the advantages of living in Mexico and take with them American constitutional freedoms and laissez faire capitalism. The final outcome of a case in the Mexican courts or of a dispute with administrative authorities often was blamed on the ambassador and, occasionally, credited to him. Clayton had an image of ineffectiveness or impassivity in his seemingly impersonal responses to the plight of various American citizens in Mexico, suggesting that they "exhaust" their judicial remedies before coming to him and then expecting them to bring evidence of an air-tight case showing a "denial of justice."[25]

One is inclined to accuse Clayton of deliberate dissimulation in view of his numerous letters claiming that he could act officially with the Mexican government only upon direct orders from the State Department. That was not true. He often acted on his own initiative. The State Department, however, considered diplomatic intervention for private citizens secondary to the primary function of official liaison between the two governments. Private citizens, on the other hand, either did not understand that or did not accept it, as a letter from an attorney indicated:

> Your answer makes it plain that instead of exercising your powers for the protection of your fellow-countrymen you have become an active assistant of those who are seeking to get possession of his money and property dishonestly under the cloak of legal proceedings . . . [under] the theory that you consider harmonious official relations of more importance than the protection of individual rights of Americans.

Clayton's temper flared, but by that time he had learned how to handle such disrespectful language towards the American ambassador. He replied:

> I am not permitted to correspond with private persons concerning matters which may be a subject of official correspondence or discussion with the government to which I am accredited.[26]

Throughout the Mealy case the State Department supported Clayton in his handling of the matter and from time to time sent him instructions. A telegram in cipher in October 1901 read: "Unless Mealy exhausts all judicial remedies and clearly shows a final denial of justice, this government could not intervene." As the case moved toward a crisis the Department reassured Clayton of its support:

> ... Your course throughout appears to have been characterized by fidelity and discretion and is approved by the Department. The Department commends your declared purpose to do for Mealy all that can properly be done, notwithstanding the somewhat trying character of his communications.[27]

Debate over another case even went to the United States Senate, where, on 30 June 1902, Senator J. W. Bailey of Texas offered a resolution calling for the official papers in the Samuel Scott case, maintaining that Scott had been unfairly treated, not only by the Mexican courts but also by Ambassador Clayton and the officials of the State Department. Senator Bailey characterized Clayton as "either dishonest or incompetent. In either case he ought to be removed." Senator Albert Beveridge of Indiana defended the State Department, saying that the Senator from Texas had made an "unwarranted attack," and several senators, including Mark Hanna, defended Ambassador Clayton. A senator from Kansas thought that Scott had been "outrageously treated," but that was no reflection on Clayton. Senator Hanna described the ambassador as his "personal friend" and thought enemies were attempting to "throw upon the character and integrity of the ambassador a cloud of suspicion."[28]

When the Senate recessed, Senator Bailey stormed over to Senator Beveridge's desk in the Senate chambers and demanded a retraction of his remarks. Beveridge assured Bailey that he meant no personal offense, but when he refused to recant, the Senator from Texas lunged at the Senator from Indiana, grabbing him by the throat and knocking over a desk in the scuffle. Several bystanding senators restrained Senator Bailey with some difficulty, who shouted as he was being led away to the cloakroom that he would "smash him in the mouth." Senator Beveridge straightened his ruffled clothing and casually passed off the incident as of no consequence. The State Department reported the episode to Ambassador Clayton and enclosed a copy of Senator Bailey's remarks in the United States Senate.[29]

Political enemies of Clayton not only sought to smear his reputation with exaggeration and distortion as in the El Carmen affair but even occasionally used complete fabrications, as when his son resigned as military attaché to the United States Embassy in Mexico City. The Baltimore *American*, under the headline, "Why Lt. Clayton Resigned," reported that young Clayton was at a Christmas party in Mexico City in 1902 and got into a heated discussion with a Mexican army officer who challenged him to a duel. Lieutenant Clayton refused the challenge and as a result lost so much "face" for cowardice among the Mexican aristocracy that he had to resign. His father wrote to Secretary Hay that there was "not a shadow of foundation" for that "malicious and mendacious report." He thought someone was trying to injure the ambassador by damaging his son's reputation. Lieutenant Clayton had left for Fort Myer on 8 August 1902 so was not in Mexico City Christmas 1902. Ambassador Clayton enclosed a clipping from the *Mexican Herald* which denied the report issued by the Associated Press and observed that the young officer had always been well-liked in Mexico City.[30]

Secretary of State John Hay's communications were usually quite proper and formal and seldom took sides on any given incident. That one was an exception:

> I have . . . communicated to the representatives of the Press Association here your contradiction of the malicious and slanderous report which has been put about in regard to your son. It is hard to understand such stupid malignity.[31]

Probably the most amusing series of correspondence criticizing Ambassador Clayton (though surely Clayton did not consider it so) was between the ambassador and Charles Dailey, the "proprietor and manager" of the Aspen *Democrat* in Aspen, Colorado, concerning the imprisonment in Mexico City of his brother-in-law, Arthur Sinclair Holly. Clayton first heard from Dailey late in March 1904, demanding an immediate investigation into why Holly was in prison:

> . . . My understanding of your position, General Clayton, is that if you use it to the welfare of your own countrymen, such wrongs will not be tolerated . . . and when you make a plea or a demand in the name of [the United States], no country on the face of the globe dare refuse it.
>
> In lieu [sic] of this fact I shall expect no excuse from you or any dilatory action as a servant of this government. . . .

Dailey informed Clayton that unless he heard at once that Clayton had taken energetic steps to secure Holly's release, he would inform an impressive list of senators, ex-senators, and the governor of Colorado and through them have the matter "fully reported to your chief, President Roosevelt."

If that was not enough, Dailey would also use his influence as a newspaperman "and pull in the aforesaid American press." He continued:

> There seems to be a general opinion prevailing in Mexico that you have lived so long in that damned country that you are fast acquiring the *mañana* principles of the natives of that country, and are continually putting off all American citizens who are unjustly treated in that country. . . .
>
> We are now upon the eve of a campaign and nothing will afford a Democratic paper . . . more pleasure than to criticize a Republican representative sent to another country.[32]

Clayton ordered one of the embassy secretaries to investigate the matter and discovered that Arthur Holly was in jail for falsification of signatures on insurance acceptances; that he was well-satisfied with his lawyer; that he had been, according to his own testimony, treated with "every consideration and fairness"; and that Holly had not asked for diplomatic intervention because he had not been denied any of the rights accorded to him under Mexican law. Clayton so informed Dailey and commented: "The rest of your letter, though sorely trying my patience, I prefer to pass unnoticed." Later Holly requested Clayton's assistance, but Clayton would not intervene for two reasons: the case was still on appeal, and Holly had admitted his forgery.[33]

Clayton's refusal to go to the foreign office with the case brought Dailey back into the matter. "I have this day written President Roosevelt," he informed Clayton,

> to see if you can't be made to do something in the case. I understand Mrs. Holly has done everything except to fawn at your feet in an endeavor to get you to do something.
>
> Your neglect to look after the interests of your countrymen is no doubt due to your becoming Mexicanized to the extent of believing you are a dictator in your own right. . . .

Then Dailey actually apologized for having to "call on his Chief to compel [Clayton] to do his duty." He reassured the ambassador:

> I did not abuse you in my letter to the President, as that is not my way of doing business. . . . [!]

Clayton's reply to Dailey consisted of one sentence:

> I have to acknowledge the receipt of your communication of the 22nd ultimo.[34]

Ambassador Clayton knew well that diplomacy is largely persuasive in nature and is often dependent for success on courtesy and mutual favors rather than on blustering demands and intimidation. Having held high command positions in the United States Army and high political offices such as Governor of Arkansas, he realized the distinction between issuing an authoritative order and a diplomatic request for action from another sovereign government. Astute politician that he was, Clayton knew that to be effective in political persuasion, one must be selective as to when and how often such political favors were requested. Implications in many letters indicated that many persons thought that Clayton could "do something" if he simply "wanted to." Nevertheless, the "want to" and the political expediency of a matter were often interrelated. It was not so much that Clayton did not "want to" aid distressed Americans in Mexico, for he often did. It was more that he believed he had to choose carefully the frequency and intensity of his requests, or veiled demands, to the Mexican foreign office, and, especially, to President Diaz. It was simply a question of political expedience. For example, it was imperative politically for Clayton to get what action he could from the Mexican government in the Mealy case, and he did. It was possible that Mealy would have won his case in the Mexican Supreme Court without Clayton's carefully-chosen and relatively frequent conversations with Mariscal over the matter, but the fact that the case was so narrowly decided and the court so careful to "save face" in not actually exonerating Mealy, leads one to suspect that pressure from the executive branch tilted the scales (of justice? or of politics?) in Mealy's favor. The factor which prompted Clayton to action was that it was to his benefit politically to do so. Perhaps the element of duty and a desire to perform well for his own sense of satisfaction were part of his motivation also, but so was political expediency.

Evidence of that element in Clayton's thinking was an incident involving Senator Mark Hanna, who contacted Clayton on behalf of friends who were stockholders in a Rhode Island corporation known as the Tabasco Electrical and Improvement Company. The Tabasco Company furnished electricity to several municipalities in Mexico. When one of them, the Municipality of San Juan Bautista, violated its contract by failing to pay for the lighting of the city for four consecutive months, the company refused to furnish any more electricity. In retaliation, the Governor of the State of Tabasco declared the contract forfeited since the company was not furnishing the electricity called for in the contract. The Tabasco Company, wishing to avoid litigation, requested Senator Hanna to contact Ambassador Clayton to arrange for a personal interview with

President Diaz, who, the company hoped, would be able to persuade the Governor of Tabasco to come to terms. So Hanna wrote a letter of introduction for the representatives of the company in Mexico and to Clayton:

> ... If you could arrange an audience with the president, entirely unofficial, having these gentlemen accompany you, I am convinced it would have the desired result. If my friends save anything at all, it will be through the powerful influence of President Diaz.
>
> You may be sure I shall appreciate whatever you may be able to accomplish in the matter.[35]

The ambassador complied with the senator's request. To the president of Mexico he wrote:

> Permit me to enclose a translation of a letter from the Honorable M. A. Hanna, a gentleman of much influence in the United States, as Your Excellency doubtless knows.

Clayton then requested an interview with the president, and continued:

> I regret very much to trouble Your Excellency with such matters, but as Mr. Hanna has asked for my good offices three times in this affair it is impossible for me to continue to disregard his wishes.

The ambassador received an immediate reply from the president and an appointment for a personal interview the following day.[36]

Conveniently, after a few weeks the Governor of Tabasco happened to be in Mexico City and after another interview between Clayton and Diaz, the president replied to a letter from the ambassador, addressing him as "Esteemed and distinguished friend":

> Referring to your courteous letter of yesterday, I have requested the Governor of Tabasco to remain for some days longer in this city for the object which you are pleased to indicate, notwithstanding he had already taken passage to return today. ...

The president of Mexico overruled the governor of the State of Tabasco, recognized the validity of the electrical company's claim, and negotiated a final settlement with the company to sell their contract and property within the municipality for $45,000 Mexican currency. What should be obvious is the rarity with which such arrangements could be made.[37]

As the time approached for his resignation, Ambassador Clayton attended the seventh inauguration of aging President Diaz on 1 December 1904. The Ambassador of the United States wore his army uniform and General Diaz wore plain evening clothes with the tricolor band across his chest. Clayton addressed the assembled dignitaries, praising Diaz for the "wonderful success" of his efforts to establish the national credit of Mexico. The President of Mexico, after referring to his re-election as the "renewal of the popular mandate," thanked Clayton for his "discreet" and "patriotic" representation of the United States.[38]

Ambassador Clayton was always careful with his embassy budget. By the end of his term his expenses included one hundred dollars a month rent and a larger staff: a translator, a clerk-recorder, a stenographer, an usher and copyist, a messenger, a porter, and occasionally an extra typist. Clayton's last inventory as ambassador showed some growth since 1897. He then had seven wastebaskets, ten cuspidors, and four typewriters. Clayton had embellished the originally drab embassy to include seven pairs of lace curtains and four carpets designated on the inventory as "plush." Clayton lunched with President Diaz and his family at Chapultepec Castle on 25 May 1905. The next day he was officially escorted there again by Ignacio Mariscal to present his letter of recall.[39]

Ambassador Clayton with grand-daughter Kathleen at the American Embassy in Mexico City, 1905

Clayton served as ambassador in a quiescent period in Mexican-United States relations. Mexican foreign policy decisions were compliant, designed to avoid any major diplomatic confrontation. Nevertheless, Mexico maintained jealously the sovereign rights of independence and zealously took refuge in the security of international custom. She accepted diplomatic intervention only in a very limited way.

United States foreign service positions at the turn of the century were an important patronage source for national administrations. As one would expect from such a system, Ambassador Clayton was a mediocre, amateur diplomat in a relatively minor embassy, but he performed better than might be anticipated. His personal appearance and military bearing lent dignity to his image. His political experience gave him a certain prudence and astuteness that were of value to him as an ambassador. Clayton learned and grew in his office. He was systematic and efficient, well-disciplined, and meticulously subordinate to State Department instructions. Clayton, however, did not really understand Mexican people and culture and thus took too much at face value that was presented to him by Foreign Minister Mariscal, who was a more astute and seasoned politician than Clayton. Clayton's excessive preoccupation with Arkansas and American national politics distracted him from the necessary concentration his position required. The greatest upheaval in modern Mexican history, the Revolution of 1910, began shortly after Clayton's tenure as ambassador, but his reports to the State Department give no indication that anything was amiss. His one lengthy dispatch on the internal political situation in Mexico consisted of a discussion of what Clayton perceived to be the reasons for a cabinet shake-up and possible successors to the presidency after Diaz. There was nothing to indicate that Clayton was even dimly aware of the conditions and leaders which produced a revolution just five years after he left office.

Ambassador Clayton wrote nothing of the occasional political riots which broke out during his time in Mexico, particularly in the northern tier of states, such as the riot in Monterrey on 2 April 1903 which the American consul reported to the State Department. Troops and police fired on the demonstrators and killed fifteen. The demonstrators' revolutionary "Manifesto to the Nation" complained of arbitrary government, official terrorism, and "unwarranted intermeddling in the political affairs" of Mexico by foreign businessmen. A few days later some 10,000 demonstrators marched in the streets of Monterrey and were met with a fusillade from City Hall balconies. Sixty were wounded and twelve were killed. Apparently Ambassador Clayton did not consider these things important enough to report to the State Department.[40]

Despite these significant deficiencies, Clayton's political viewpoints and his style and personality suited him well for the position of ambassador to Mexico during the Diaz era. He acted in accordance with the expectations of both the United States and Mexican governments.

Notes

[1]*The Two Republics*, May 25, 1897. *Mexican Herald*, May 24, 1897, in *Despatches from United States Ministers to Mexico, 1823-1906*, Department of State, Washington, D. C., Record Group 59, M97, volume 130.

[2]*Despatches*, volume 130, number 3.

[3]*Despatches*, volume 130, number 1, May 6, 1897; 105, September 14, 1897; 244, February 22, 1897.

[4]John Sherman to Powell Clayton, October 27, 1897, John Hay to Powell Clayton, *Despatches* 50, 54, 93, 159, 505, 560.

[5]*Despatches*, volume 133, number 259, 381, 393, 11, 385, 437, 480, 427, 435, 515, 527.

[6]*Despatches*, volume 133, number 398, 496, 526, 559, 40, 515, 562, 236, 320, 357, 412, 449.

[7]*Mexican Herald*, September 17, 1898. *Despatches*, 708.

[8]J. Lloyd Mecham, *The United States and Inter-American Security, 1889-1960* (Austin: U of Texas P, 1961), 48-63. *Despatches*, 319, 347.

[9]*Despatches*, Number 2213, March 26, 1904, 2277, May 9, 1904.

[10]*Diplomatic Instructions of the Department of State, 1801-1906: Mexico*, Department of State, Washington, D. C., Record Group 59, M77, number 982, October 30, 1903. Governor of Oaxaca to Mexican Foreign Minister, September 3, 1904, *Despatches* 2596, December 31, 1904.

[11]*Mexican Herald*, February 21, 1904. *Despatches*, 2112, 2165, 2166.

[12]Powell Clayton to Ignacio Mariscal, *Despatches*, 1638, November 25, 1902.

[13]*Despatches*, 1762, March 31, 1903, 2061, December 4, 1903.

[14]*Notes from the Mexican Legation in the United States to the Department of State, 1821-1906*, Department of State, Washington, D. C., Record Group 59, M54, December 28, 1896, and July 11, 1899.

[15]*Instructions*, volume 25, telegram in cipher, November 16, 1901, November 27, 1901.

[16]*Despatches*, volume 167, Confidential no number, January 18, 1904. Daniel Cosio Villegas, *American Extremes* (Austin: U of Texas P, 1964), 39. Carleton Beals, *Porfirio Diaz: Dictator of Mexico* (Philadelphia: J. B. Lippincott, 1932), 256.

[17]*Despatches*, volume 167, April 1, 1904.

[18]*Instructions* 622, December 27, 1901. Francis J. Weber, "The Pious Fund of the Californias," *Hispanic American Historical Review*, XLIII (1963), 79ff.

[19]*Despatches* 1192, December 1, 1904. *Instructions* 274, January 5, 1900, 552, June 3, 1902, October 4, 1904 to April 27, 1905. *Mexican Legation* 242, December 22, 1897.

[20]*Despatches* 2609, January 18, 1905, and 2798, May 17, 1905.

[21]*Despatches* 1114, 1192, Decision of First Circuit Court, March 29, 1902, *Despatches* 1326, 1135, 1154, 1204, 1270, 1266.

[22]"Argument before Appellate Court in Mexico in defense of W. H. Mealy, November, 1901," *Despatches* 1194. The New York *Times*, April 14, 1902.

[23]*Arkansas Gazette*, March 14, 15, 1902.

[24]*Despatches* 1503, July 29, 1902. *Mexican Herald*, July 29, 1902. Telegram in cipher, January 12, 1903, *Despatches*, volume 161, number 1695, January 28, 1903.

[25]An example of the attitude described was reflected in a protest from the State Department to the Mexican government protesting a Mexican law requiring the registration of traveling salesmen in Mexico on the grounds that no such requirement existed in the United States. Clayton to Harle, February 29, 1904, and Richardson to Clayton, November 28, 1904, *Despatches*, 2562. Clayton to Richardson, December 8, 1904, *Despatches*, 2562.

[26]Nicholson and Mullally to Clayton, January 23, 1902, Clayton to Nicholson and Mullally, February 1, 1902, *Despatches*, 1312.

[27]*Instructions*, volume 25, October 12, 1901, Hay to Clayton, November 2, 1901, *Instructions*, 597.

[28]*Washington Post*, July 1, 1902. The *Arkansas Gazette*, July 1, 1902. *Despatches*, 1620.

[29]*Ibid.*

[30]*Despatches*, volume 155, March 19, 1902.

[31]Hay to Clayton, March 24, 1902, *Instructions*, volume 25.

[32]Dailey to Clayton, March, 1904, *Despatches*, 2223.

[33]Clayton to Dailey, April 2, 1904, *Despatches*, 2223, 2386.

[34]Dailey to Clayton, September 22, 1904, *Despatches*, 2461, Dailey to Clayton, October 4, 1904, *Despatches*, 2461, 2514.

[35]Mark Hanna to Powell Clayton, July 6, 1901, *Despatches*, 1252.

[36]Powell Clayton to Porfirio Diaz, August 12, 1901, *Despatches*, 1252.

[37]Porfirio Diaz to Powell Clayton, December 20, 1901, *Despatches*, 1252.

[38]*Mexican Herald*, December 2, 1904, *Despatches*, 2604.

[39]*Despatches*, 2604, 2814, 2726, 2800, 2813.

[40]Charles Curtis Cumberland, *Mexican Revolution: Genesis under Madero* (Austin: U of Texas P, 1952), 14-15. Phillip Hanna to Francis B. Loomis, Assistant Secretary of State, April 3, 1903, *Consuls Monterrey*, 150, 153, April 29, 1903. Jose F. Godoy, *Porfiro Diaz: President of Mexico* (New York: G. P. Putnam's Sons, 1910), 138.

Chapter Seven

POWELL CLAYTON

Powell Clayton's ancestry and family experiences prepared him for a predominantly political career. The Claytons were always conscious of their lineage and traditions, tracing their origins to Claytown in Sussex, England. Powell Clayton's line of the family came from Thomas Clayton, owner of "Clayton Hall" in Yorkshire in 1560, and from William of Chichester, who moved to Pennsylvania with William Penn in 1671. He brought the family coat of arms with him, inscribed with the legend, *Probitatem quam divitias*, meaning "Honor rather than wealth."

The name *Powell* entered the family through the maiden name of Powell Clayton's great-grandmother. His grandfather, the first Powell Clayton, was not involved in politics and, "therefore," according to one of his grandsons, "led a comparatively happy life and died a peaceful death, loved and respected by all who knew him." The same could not be said of his namesake.

Powell Clayton's father, John, inherited the family farm near Bethel, Pennsylvania, where Powell and his brothers grew up. Their father raised mostly fruit: apples, cherries, and peaches. "A staunch Jeffersonian Democrat," he named his eldest son Thomas Jefferson Clayton because he was born on 26 July 1826, just three weeks after the death of the former President. A few years later John Clayton joined the Whig party in opposition to the Jacksonians and in 1840 was a delegate to the Whig National Convention in Baltimore, which nominated William Henry Harrison for President and John Tyler for Vice-President. The Claytons had twin sons that year whom they named William Henry Harrison Clayton and John Tyler Clayton. When President Harrison died and Vice-President John Tyler "treacherously" abandoned his party, John Clayton expunged the name "Tyler" from the family record and had his infant son baptized John Middleton Clayton, after a relative who lived in Delaware.[1]

Powell Clayton continued the tradition of political combativeness and exaggerated party loyalty from his father. Indeed, the entire family seemed to accept the same principles, as the writings and careers of all the Clayton brothers indicated. Six of the Clayton children died in childhood. Only the four brothers survived and each followed a political career. Thomas Jefferson Clayton was an attorney and judge in Pennsylvania. William Henry Harrison Clayton became a circuit judge and then United States District Attorney in Fort Smith, Arkansas. John Middleton Clayton was sheriff of Jefferson County, Arkansas, and the presiding officer of the Arkansas Senate. He was murdered while seeking a Congressional seat.[2]

Confrontational politics was the Clayton style. Conciliatory, empathetic, and compromising the Claytons were not. The most conciliatory member of the family was the mother, Ann Clark Clayton. Her father was a British colonial army officer and a Tory until he died in 1812, much to the embarrassment of the maternal side of her family who were staunch American patriots all. Ann Clayton tried, apparently without much success, to persuade her sons that the way they were brought up had influenced their political beliefs more than philosophical arguments and persuasion, that "interest" was more significant in politics than "ideology." In the heat of the campaign of 1840 she commented to her oldest son, "Have you ever thought that if your father had been a *Loco Foco*, you would perhaps, be one?" He did not believe her. Neither did Powell Clayton later.[3]

Powell Clayton's mother was the daughter of an "enemy" soldier. So was his wife. Clayton married Adaline McGraw of Helena, Arkansas, the daughter of a steamboat captain, John (Ben) McGraw, who served as a major in the Confederate army. His ho-

tel was taken over by Union officers and Adaline apparently met Powell under those circumstances. A persistent tale is that Colonel Clayton once arrested Adaline for her defiant behavior, for she was a spirited Southern lass. Adaline was born in Paducah, Kentucky, on 26 January 1843 and married Clayton on 14 December 1865. Judging from the few letters and other historical records that have survived, Clayton and his wife apparently did not have a particularly close relationship. Adaline devoted her life to her children and to various civic activities, particularly in Eureka Springs. At times she was quite out-

Adaline McGraw Clayton
Photo: Ann Westfall

spoken within the family, protesting her husband's risky business ventures. She predicted, for instance, that the Crescent Hotel would prove "to be a white elephant which will not pay." She played the part of a traditional Victorian housewife who addressed her husband formally and kept family matters private, but at times she must have been a bit difficult for her stern and dignified husband. For example, she wrote to a friend during the Spanish-American War that the United States should have "kept their fingers out of the pie! General Clayton thinks it dreadful the way I feel and think and has forbidden me expressing my opinions outside of the family. . . ."[4]

Charlotte Clayton

The Claytons had five children: Lucy, Powell, Jr., Charlotte, Kathleen, and Glover, who died in infancy. Lucy, born in 1868, married young and was widowed at the age of twenty-two. She later married Samuel Jones, who eventually became a brigadier general in the United States Army. She died in California in 1929 and left no children. Powell Clayton, Jr., born in 1871, pursued a military career. He was military attaché for his father in Mexico City and was later stationed in Washington, D. C. He had a congenial, cheerful personality and, like his father, loved the military life. His wife was Nancy Langhorne from Virginia. They had no children. Kathleen, the youngest, was born in 1878 and at the age of twenty-eight married Sir Arthur Grant-Duff and accompanied him in his British diplomatic career to Cuba, Germany, South America, and Sweden. Kathleen, like her brother and sister Lucy, had no children but was very fond of her sister Charlotte's children. Kathleen was a good-looking, "elegant" woman, intelligent and amusing. She was cheerful and had the ability to make light of many situations in life. During the First World War she gave lodging and encouragement to her sister Charlotte, whose husband was away in the Belgian diplomatic service.

Charlotte Clayton met her husband, the Belgian Minister to Mex-

Charlotte Clayton with daughter
Kathleen and son Charles Moncheur

ico, Baron Ludovic Moncheur, while her father was United States Minister to Mexico. A widower, he was some twenty years her senior. The Baroness Moncheur lived an active and eventful life in Mexico City, Washington, D. C., Belgium, Constantinople, and England. Baron Moncheur was in the highest political circles of Belgium, and his wife, a charming, gracious, and vivacious woman, was equal to the role she was expected to play. Charlotte's photographs and family reminiscences reveal a strikingly beautiful woman with gray-green eyes and dark hair, a rather round face, and a lovely mouth. She was tall and dignified, well-educated, very intelligent, and a witty conversationalist. She played bridge well and delighted in winning money from European royalty. The Baroness was a long-time friend and correspondent of Chief Justice Oliver Wendell Holmes and delved deeply into history and philosophy. Despite the many separations occasioned by a diplomatic career, the Moncheurs lived a reasonably happy life and had three children, Powell Clayton's only grandchildren: Kathleen Adaline (obviously named for Charlotte's sister and mother), Charles, and Marie. Clayton's only grandson, Charles Moncheur, carried on the family military tradition by serving in the Royal Air Force during World War II. He survived fifty-nine bombing missions over Germany. Kathleen de Montpellier died in 1983 at her lovely gardens of Annevoie in

Charlotte Clayton Moncheur's
Castle at Nameche, Belgium.

Belgium. All of Powell Clayton's descendants, then, are European, living in Belgium and England.[5]

Adaline Clayton maintained a close relationship with her children as adults, but was not impressed with the fact that two of them had married into European nobility. A family photograph taken at Charlotte's wedding showed her mother sitting with her lips tightly compressed, "austerely dressed," and with her hair pinned up in a bun—evidently not concerned with current fashion. She intensely disliked being apart from her children and was perhaps too possessive of them. Years later she wrote, "The separations in life have always been to me one of its saddest phases and Charlotte's going is an awful blow. . . ." Adaline wrote regularly to her children, particularly to her son, with whom she corresponded almost daily throughout his adult

Gardens and castle of Annevoie, Belgium where Kathleen Moncheur, Clayton's granddaughter, lived. Pictured with author's wife, Minnie, (center) is Clayton's grandson, Vincent Goffinet, and his wife Joelle.

life. Powell, Jr., survived his father by only two years. While commanding a cavalry squadron in 1916 at Fort Sam Houston in San Antonio, Texas he was thrown from a horse and died from his injuries a short time later. His death was so sudden that his mother never recovered from the shock. She had gone to England to visit her daughter Kathleen after the death of her husband. The trauma of her son's death apparently was too much for her. According to her granddaughter, she simply "gave up" and died two weeks later in Limpsfield, Surrey, England, about thirty miles south of London.[6]

In contrast to his wife, Powell Clayton was an exceptionally private individual. He kept his family life completely separate from his public activities. He seldom mentioned anything about his family, not even in letters to close political friends. His was a sort of bifurcated existence. He was well aware of the various roles he was expected to play and apparently kept those roles distinct within his own mind. In his family role he felt a fierce sense of loyalty and responsibility. Often he provided jobs or material support to relatives temporarily in need of help. Always manipulative, Clayton tried to maneuver his children into marrying "upward," socially and financially. He loved his children, sought to protect them, and wanted to be near them as adults. He was enraged during a minor incident in Mexico City when police harassed two of his daughters as they rode about in a carriage. He managed to secure his son's appointment as military attaché when he was ambassador and his son-in-law's military transfer to Washington, D. C., after Clayton moved there. He accompanied his daughter Charlotte to Europe in the summer of 1903 and wrote her that he hoped her baby would be "as great a comfort" to her father as she had always been to hers. Though never noted for his wealth or generosity, Clayton bequeathed $25,000 to each of his children which he "advanced" to them long before his death. After his retirement to Washington, however, family letters occasionally complained of his cantankerousness and the difficulty of getting along with him in daily life. A helpful expedient was to find someone with whom he liked to play cards or Parcheesi. Clayton had a violent temper. He hated losing at cards and sometimes became quite angry when he did. Many were afraid of his forceful personality and most tried to placate his volatile moods.[7]

As so often happens to older men, however, the presence of his grandchildren brought out a certain gentleness and sentimentality that Clayton seldom expressed except to them. That was a side of his personality that few knew about and fewer saw. One wonders how many of his political friends, and enemies as well, would have been shocked to read a letter he once wrote to his five-year old granddaughter, Kathleen, who had been born in his home in Washington, D. C., in 1904 and who was his favorite:

> . . . I am going to keep your letter always to remind me of my little girl and the happy time we had together at York Harbor. After you left, I missed you so much. The tears sometimes moistened my eyes when taking my afternoon walks. I saw the rocks we used to climb and the many spots where in so many different ways we used to amuse each other. I have before me on my desk one of the little stones you gave me for a paper weight. Grangran [Grandma] and I often kiss it because your dear little fingers once surrounded it. It too will I always keep before me on my desk to remind me every day of my little girl and the happy summer days we spent together at York Harbor. . . .

"Dada" was the name Kathleen and the other grandchildren called Clayton. He called her "Little K." His own children called him "Pappy."[8]

Clayton's lack of candor and his ability to dissimulate make it difficult to reconstruct a coherent view of the guiding assumptions and purposes of his life. His world view and value system, particularly his political philosophy, were reflected in what he did and said, but he was neither a meditative nor expressive person and most of those very significant matters must be dealt with by implication and by induction, if at all. Very little has survived in the written record concerning Powell Clayton's beliefs.

Clayton was an authoritarian, dictatorial type of person who could be friendly and helpful only as long as he was convinced of the other person's "loyalty." One of Clayton's political opponents was not totally inaccurate when he claimed that every Arkansas Republican had to follow "the rotten scoundrel Clayton, or else be pronounced *persona non grata*" by the party leadership. He was so authoritarian that he counselled Remmel not even to have a Vice-Chairman of the party: "There should be but one head of the committee, and then there is no danger of clashes or inharmonious action." Clayton saw "danger in divided authority." If the vice-chairman was not "in full accord" with the chairman, he might "take advantage" of the chairman's temporary absence to "disorganize" the party interests. No doubt Clayton remembered Lieutenant Governor Johnson's "attempted coup" when as Governor of Arkansas, Clayton left the state for a brief time.

One wonders just how paranoid Clayton actually was and whether he completely trusted anyone. Certainly he always kept his own counsel and his mouth shut. He was vague and evasive and tried to keep the opposition (which he always had) guessing as to his next course of action. Even in a relatively candid letter to Remmel, Clayton was obscure and mysterious:

> I will manage to have a conference with our friends and arrive at a future program. I have several "cards" up my sleeve, which I do not care to play until the proper time comes.

Clayton was a gambler, not only at cards and in various business schemes, but also in his choices in life. He put his whole energy into a project and often pursued elusive goals relentlessly, as if he were going for "double or nothing." He abandoned an objective only when he finally realized the game was over.[9]

Never a reformer and usually defending the status quo, Clayton's principal purpose in life seemed to be to achieve political success, which he interpreted as holding office, either within the government or within the party. He was more interested in power and prestige for its own sake than for monetary emoluments. He was quite capable of making minor adjustments to his principles and policies to accommodate himself to new political realities. He did so when Roosevelt succeeded McKinley and again when Taft succeeded Roosevelt as President. There was a certain consistency to those "adjustments," however. Clayton believed that an incoming political chief had the right to set his principles and policies in a hierarchical pattern which the lower members of the party echelon would be obliged to follow. Acquisition of a political office implied loyalty to the rest of the political team. Perhaps that is why Clayton supported Taft in 1912 rather than Roosevelt.

Nevertheless, it would be inaccurate to describe Clayton as "unprincipled," concerned only with political power and motivated only by his own "interests." To his few basic principles he clung with the tenacity of a reformer. Among those principles were loyalty, dependability, and a sense of responsibility. He was elitist in mentality but accepted a certain *noblesse oblige* as part of his elitism. He had a high standard of honor as well as an attitude of superiority toward those he considered socially inferior. Clayton was sincerely outraged at violations of political and civil rights of blacks, for example, though he did not consider blacks socially his equal. Because those violations also impaired Clayton's own political position, it was easy to charge him with hypocrisy or insincerity. But one might disagree with Clayton's political philosophy or his authoritarian elitist style and still give him credit for his accomplishments, some of which, at least, were beneficial to his society. Clayton was an opportunist, but not a hypocrite.

If Clayton used any of his various political positions or political influence improperly to enrich himself financially in more than an indirect way, he managed to keep such underhanded dealings so well hidden that no one was ever able to substantiate charges of political corruption against him, despite the desire of many to do so. Sources such as the *Arkansas Gazette* grudgingly acknowledged his financial integrity. Indeed, one could argue persuasively that the desire for political influence and power were higher on Clayton's value scale than money, and he was well aware of how scandal could destroy one's political fortunes.

The Clayton coat of arms carried the Christian cross at the center of the shield, but it did not occupy a similar place in Powell Clayton's life. Religion was something more to be tolerated than believed. His family background was Quaker and his parents were active Methodists. Clayton's mother in particular taught tolerance to her children, explaining to them that "forms of worship were but paper walls dividing Christian denominations [which] worshipped the same God and trusted in the same Sav-

ior, and that [they] should be careful to say nothing that would offend others in their religious faith." The latter part of her advice, at least, Powell Clayton followed. Indeed, not only did he not offend others in their religious views, he said virtually nothing about religion at all. In political speeches Clayton occasionally employed the pious allusions typical of the civil religion of the times, but one must question seriously whether he really believed in the implications of what he said. For example, Clayton referred in his inaugural address to God "who holds the destinies of nations in his hands."
His Thanksgiving Day proclamation in 1870 included the comment that "It behooves us at all times to make a humble acknowledgement to Almighty God for His mercies, as also of our utter dependence upon Him. . . ." And in an impassioned civil rights speech in the United States Senate, the Senator from Arkansas concluded eloquently, ". . . I hope and trust that . . . God may so order events, that . . . peace, security, and equal rights prevail all over this country. . . ." One can hardly believe that Powell Clayton was expressing a genuine belief in the sovereign control of God over human history. Those examples sound more like cultural accretions than expressions of faith when one considers them in the total context of Clayton's life.[10]

Clayton was not a member of any church although his wife attended the Episcopal Church. In 1880 a journalist explained that Clayton believed one church was about as good as another. Although he thought religion socially beneficial, he felt that it changed as men became "more enlightened." As a child, Clayton had been orthodox, accepting uncritically the teachings of his parents. By middle age "his whole theory of religion" was that it must be "adapted to man's well-being here upon earth, without reference to what is to come hereafter"—a theology as imprecise as it was unorthodox.[11]

Clayton possessed a narrowly legalistic mind. His experiences in

Arkansas taught him well that one could not automatically expect "justice" from courts of law. He understood the role of political pressures in some court decisions. Nevertheless, he also clearly saw the need for some political machinery for settling disputes as being foundational for any orderly society. Thus, as he grew older, he tended to equate "justice" and "legal procedure," hoping that the best interests of most of the people would be served in the tensions produced in a democratic society among the various branches of the government and within a given administration or legislative body. Clayton was a politician and believed that those who were willing to pay the price of being politically active in their society should also reap the privileges afforded by that involvement. The real elite to Clayton were the politically successful minority, his kind of people.

Notes

[1]Thomas J. Clayton, *Rambles and Reflections at Home and Abroad* (Chester, Penn., 1892).

[2]See Chapter Five. United States House of Representatives, *Clayton vs. Breckinridge.* 51st Cong., 1st Sess., 1890, Report #2912. John W. LeBosquet, "William Henry Harrison Clayton: A Biographical Sketch" (unpublished manuscript, Wichita, KS, n.d.).

[3]Thomas J. Clayton, *Rambles.*

[4]Peggy Jacoway, *First Ladies of Arkansas* (Kingsport, TN: Southern Publishers, 1941). Adaline Clayton to Cornelia Luce, n.d., 1898, quoted in the *Arkansas Gazette*, April 6, 1979.

[5]Notes given to the author by Diane Medlicott, great-granddaughter of Powell Clayton, n.d., Powell Clayton Papers, Special Collections, U of Arkansas, Fayetteville. Diane Medlicott and Ronald Medlicott to William H. Burnside, July 15, 1982, private collection. (Earlier Charlotte had wanted to marry the American novelist, John William Fox, Jr., but her father refused the proposal because Fox "did not earn enough money.")

[6]*Ibid.* Conversation of the author with Kathleen Moncheur, June, 1980, and with Diane Medlicott, March, 1981.

[7]Powell Clayton to Charlotte Moncheur, August 12, 1909, Powell Clayton Papers, Special Collections, University of Arkansas, Fayetteville. "Last Will and Testament of Powell Clayton," February 14, 1903, with Codicils dated December 31, 1909, January 1, 1905, and March 5, 1914, Powell Clayton Papers, Special Collections, U of Arkansas, Fayetteville.

[8]Powell Clayton to Kathleen Moncheur, September 10, 1909, Powell Clayton Papers, Special Collections, U of Arkansas, Fayetteville.

[9]*Marion Herald*, August 1, 1901, Pratt Remmel Papers, Special Collections, U of Arkansas, Fayetteville. Clayton to Remmel, September 22, 1900, October 23, 1899, Harmon Remmel Papers, Special Collections, U of Arkansas, Fayetteville. Conversation of the author with Kathleen Moncheur, June, 1980. Medlicott to Burnside, July 15, 1982.

POWELL CLAYTON • 125

[10]Thomas J. Clayton, *Rambles*, 410-11. *Congressional Record*, 43d Cong., 2d Sess., Dec. 22, 1874, III, pt. 1, 531.

[11]*The Encyclopedia of the New West* (Marshall, TX: United States Biographical Publishing, 1881), 128.

EPILOGUE

When Powell Clayton left Mexico, he did not return to Arkansas. He moved instead to Washington, D. C., where he lived the rest of his life. He remained a member of the Republican national committee and continued to control federal patronage in Arkansas. The state central committee consistently obtained both his advice and consent before presenting its recommendations for appointments to the national administration. As late as 1912 President William Howard Taft still wrote such messages as the following to the old general: "Whom do you wish appointed as postmaster at Pine Bluff?"[1]

Clayton supported Taft and worked for him as he had his predecessors. That support was no doubt significant in the stormy 1912 Republican national convention in which Clayton headed the Arkansas delegation. Earlier, violence had erupted at the Arkansas Republican state convention between Roosevelt and Taft supporters, but the "Clayton-Remmel delegates" had retained control. In May Taft wrote to Clayton:

I . . . rely on your assistance. We have certainly 570 votes now.[2]

That seemed an appropriate time for Clayton to ask the President to transfer his son-in-law to general staff headquarters in Washington. "If you will recall the conversation I had with you on January 25," Clayton wrote Taft, "it was on account of family reasons that I wanted my daughter near us." The general's son-in-law was brought to Washington as requested and promoted to major.[3]

Not long after President Woodrow Wilson's election in 1912 and the return of a Democratic national administration for the first time in sixteen years, Powell Clayton resigned as Republican national committeeman from Arkansas, a position he had held for almost forty years. An Arkansas Republican state convention expressed appreciation for Clayton's "untiring efforts" on behalf of the state party in Washington. The convention resolution credited Clayton's "integrity, his forceful personality, and his broad grasp of national affairs" for Arkansas' "being held in such high favor by repeated national Republican administrations." Harmon L. Remmel succeeded Clayton as national committeeman from Arkansas.[4]

Clayton spent the remaining months of his life in Washington and died there on 25 August 1914 at the age of eighty-one. Following private funeral services, he was buried in Arlington Cemetery with military honors. His *New York Times* obituary characterized Powell Clayton as a "distinguished statesman, diplomat, and soldier."[5]

Powell Clayton aspired to be part of the American aristocracy of power that controlled political and economic decisions in a dynamic and changing nineteenth-century America. He was part of an old, respected family that had participated in the establishing of America, but he was not born into wealth or within a locus of power. What he accomplished, he did by means of his tenacity, courage, initiative, political manipulation, and forceful, dignified, persuasive personality. He was an ambitious, natural leader who sought the adulation of those a bit lower in the hierarchy of power. He loved the praise of men and carried the titles of "General" and "Governor" throughout his life with soldierly dignity.

Notes

[1]William Howard Taft to Powell Clayton, September 12, 1912, William Howard Taft Papers.

[2]Taft to Clayton, May 22, June 24, 1912, Taft Papers.

[3]Clayton to Taft, June, 1912, Taft Papers.

[4]"Record of proceedings of Arkansas Republican Conventions, 1908-1912," n.d., Pratt Remmel Papers, Special Collections, University of Arkansas, Fayetteville.

[5]*New York Times*, August 26, 1914.

Sources

Most of Powell Clayton's personal records have not survived. They were inherited by his son and when he died, his widow had custody of them. Her relatives have not been able to locate any surviving documents from Powell Clayton, Sr.'s, life. The Clayton side of the family has contributed letters and other documents to the Powell Clayton Papers in Special Collections at the University of Arkansas in Fayetteville, but the holdings are sparse. More voluminous are the records of the Arkansas Republican Party (the Harmon L. Remmel Papers and the Pratt Remmel Papers), also in Special Collections at the University of Arkansas library. Powell Clayton wrote one book which has recently been reprinted, *The Aftermath of the Civil War in Arkansas* (New York: Neale Publishing Company, 1915). It dealt almost exclusively with his gubernatorial career. The Arkansas History Commission in Little Rock has public records for Clayton's gubernatorial years, including the *Clayton Letterbook* which contains official gubernatorial correspondence. The significant Arkansas History Commission holdings on Powell Clayton are on microfilm at the University of Arkansas library in Fayetteville.

Chapter One: Military Career. The principal sources for Clayton's military career were *The War of the Rebellion: A Compilation of the Official Records of the Union and Confederate Armies* (70 vols. in 128, Washington, 1880-1901) and the Kansas Adjutant General's Office, *Military History of Kansas Regiments During the War for the Suppression of The Great Rebellion* (Leavenworth, KS: W. S. Burke, 1870). Micropublished in *Western Americana: Frontier History of the Trans-Mississippi West, 1550-1900* (New Haven, CT: Research Publications, 1975, Reel 294, No. 2948). The Kansas State Historical Commission houses that collection and other material on the Kansas First Infantry and the Kansas Fifth Cavalry regiments. For the early history of Leavenworth see H. Miles Moore, *Early History of Leavenworth City and County* (Leavenworth, KS: Samuel Dodsworth, 1906) and Jesse A. Hall, *et al.*, *History of Leavenworth County, Kansas* (Topeka, KS: Historical Publishing Co., 1921). More useful are the Leavenworth newspapers available on microfilm at the Kansas State Historical Commission in Topeka, especially the Leavenworth *Times*, 1857-1862.

Particularly insightful for Clayton's military career was the *Diary of William F. Creitz, Commander of Company A, Fifth Kansas Cavalry, 11 September 1861 to 11 August 1864.* Kansas State Historical Society, Topeka, KS. *Report of the Adjutant General of the State of Kansas, 1861-1865.* Volume I. (Topeka: Kansas State Printing Co., 1896). For an understanding of the peculiar nature of the Civil War in Kansas, Missouri, and Arkansas, see the following: Albert Castel, *A Frontier State at War: Kansas, 1861-1865* (Ithaca, NY: American Historical Association, 1958). Jay Monaghan, *Civil War on the Western Border, 1854-1865* (New York: Bonanza Books, 1955). Stephen Z. Starr, *Jennison's Jayhawkers: A Civil War Cavalry Regiment and Its Commander* (Baton Rouge: LSU Press, 1973). Michael Fellman, *Inside War: The Guerrilla Conflict in Missouri During the American Civil War* (New York: Oxford UP, 1989). Elmo Ingenthron, *Borderland Rebellion: A History of the Civil War on the Missouri-Arkansas Border* (Branson, MO: Ozarks Mountaineer, 1980). For the Robinson/Lane political competition see Wendell H. Stephenson, *The Political Career of General James H. Lane* (Topeka: Publications of the Kansas State Historical Society, 1930) and Don W. Wilson, *Governor Charles Robinson of Kansas* (Lawrence: UP of Kansas, 1975). For the broader historical context that Clayton dealt with see Ira Don Richards, "The Battle of Poison Spring," *Arkansas Historical*

Quarterly, XVIII (1959), his "The Engagement at Marks' Mills," *AHQ*, XIX (1960), and Leo E. Huff, "The Union Expedition Against Little Rock, August-September 1863" *AHQ*, XXII (1973). For the Confederate side see Bobby L. Roberts, "General T. C. Hindman and the Trans-Mississippi District," *AHQ*, XXXII (1973). Helpful monographs were Stephen Z. Starr, *The Union Cavalry in the Civil War*, Volume III:*The War in the West, 1861-1865* (Baton Rouge: LSU Press, 1985), and Ludwell H. Johnson, *Red River Campaign: Politics and Cotton in the Civil War* (Baltimore: Johns Hopkins, 1958). There are many articles on the Civil War in the *Arkansas Historical Quarterly*, the two most significant of which for Clayton's role were both by Edwin C. Bearss, "The Battle of Helena, July 4, 1863," XX (1961), and "Marmaduke Attacks Pine Bluff," XXIII (1964). *The Kansas Historical Quarterly* is useful for life in the 1855-1861 period in Kansas.

Chapter Two: Gubernatorial Career. Besides Clayton's *Aftermath* and *Letterbook*, the *Arkansas Gazette* provided invaluable information, as did many *Arkansas Historical Quarterly* articles, especially Otis A. Singletary, "Militia Disturbances in Arkansas During Reconstruction," XV (1956), and Orval Truman Driggs, Jr., "The Issues of the Powell Clayton Regime, 1868-1871," VIII (1949). The standard work for many years on Arkansas politics during Reconstruction was Thomas S. Staples, *Reconstruction in Arkansas, 1862-1874* (Gloucester, MA: Peter Smith, 1923). Important recent interpretive articles on the militia were Michael P. Kelley, "Partisan or Protector: Powell Clayton and the 1868 Presidential Election," *The Ozark Historical Review*, III (1974), and Howard C. Westwood, "The Federals' Cold Shoulder to Arkansas' Powell Clayton," *Civil War History*, XXVI (1980). The most comprehensive scholarly work on the Ku Klux Klan was Allen W. Trelease, *White Terror: The Ku Klux Klan Conspiracy and Southern Reconstruction* (New York: Harper and Row, 1971), which contained a chapter entitled, "The Arkansas Militia vs. the Ku Klux Klan." A significant portion of the United States Congress investigating committee's 1871 report on *Affairs in the Late Insurrectionary States: The Ku Klux Conspiracy* dealt with Arkansas. An important recent work dealing with this period of Arkansas history is John I. Smith, *Forward from Rebellion: Reconstruction and Revolution in Arkansas, 1868-1874* (Little Rock: Rose Publishing, 1983).

Useful in analyzing financial and social issues during the Clayton administration were Carter Goodrich, "Public Aid to Railroads in the Reconstruction South," *Political Science Quarterly*, LXXI (1956); Bessie Carter Randolph, "Foreign Bondholders and the Repudiated Debts of the Southern States," *American Journal of International Law*, XXV (1931); William Clarence Evans, "The Public Debt of Arkansas: Its History from 1836 to 1885," unpublished M.A. thesis, U of Arkansas, 1928; Dallas T. Herndon, "Repudiation or Thumbing the Nose—Which?: The Story Back of the 'Holford Bonds' and 'The Fishback Amendment,'" *Arkansas Historical Review*, I (1934); Martha A. Ellenburg, "Reconstruction in Arkansas," unpublished Ph.D. dissertation, U. of Missouri, 1967; and, especially, George H. Thompson, *Arkansas and Reconstruction:The Influence of Geography, Economics and Personality* (Port Washington, NY: Kennikat, 1967). Many *Arkansas Historical Quarterly* articles were helpful, including Garland E. Bayliss, "Post-Reconstruction Repudiation: Evil Blot or Financial Necessity?" XXIII (1964), and Stephen E. Wood, "The Development of Arkansas Railroads," VII (1948).

To fit this aspect of Arkansas history into its broader Southern context, see Robert C. Morris, *Reading, 'Riting, and Reconstruction* (Chicago: U of Chicago P, 1981), and Mark W. Summers, *Railroads, Reconstruction, and the Gospel of Prosperity: Aid Under the Radical Republicans, 1865-1877* (Princeton, NJ: Princeton UP, 1984).

For the attempted impeachment of Governor Powell Clayton by the Arkansas General Assembly, see Arkansas General Assembly, *Proceedings in the House of Representatives of Arkansas in the Case of the Impeachment of Governor Powell Clayton* (Little Rock: Price and Baron, 1871), and Cortez A. M. Ewing, "Arkansas Reconstruction Impeachments," *Arkansas Historical Quarterly*, XIII (1954).

Chapter Three: Senatorial Career. Sources were primarily the *Congressional Globe* (through the 42d Congress) and the *Congressional Record* (beginning with the 43d Congress). The United States Senate published separately *Report of the Special Committee to Inquire into Certain Allegations Against Honorable Powell Clayton* (42d Congress, 3d Session, 1872). Everette Swinney discussed those allegations in his "United States v. Powell Clayton: Use of the Federal Enforcement Acts in Arkansas," *Arkansas Historical Quarterly*, XXVI (1967). His role in the Brooks-Baxter war was seen in James Atkinson, "The Brooks-Baxter Contest," *Arkansas Historical Quarterly*, IV (1945) and in Earl Woodward, "The Brooks and Baxter War in Arkansas, 1872-1874," XXX (1971).

Recent interpretations of reconstruction in general are Richard N. Current, *Those Terrible Carpetbaggers* (Oxford UP, 1988), William Gillette, *Retreat from Reconstruction: 1869-1879* (Baton Rouge: LSU Press, 1979), and Eric Foner, *Reconstruction: America's Unfinished Revolution: 1863-1877* (New York: Harper & Row, 1988).

Chapter Four: Business Career. Clayton's role in building the Eureka Springs Railroad was synthesized from James R. Fair, Jr., *The North Arkansas Line: The Story of the Missouri and North Arkansas Railroad* (Berkeley, CA: Howell-North, 1969) and in building the town of Eureka Springs from June Westphal and Catharine Osterhage, *A Fame Not Easily Forgotten* (Conway, AR, 1970). Helpful sources were scattered issues of the Eureka Springs *Daily Times-Echo*; Cora Pinkley-Call, *Pioneer Tales of Eureka Springs and Carroll County* (Eureka Springs, AR,1930); and Oklute Braswell, ed., *History of Carroll County, Arkansas* (Berryville, AR: Braswell Printing, 1889). Several letters from the Powell Clayton Papers were also useful, as were scattered issues of the *Arkansas Gazette*.

Chapter Five: Republican Party Career. The basic source of materials for Clayton's political career were the records of the Arkansas Republican Party (Harmon L. Remmel Papers and the Pratt Remmel Papers). The Presidential papers for each of the Republican Presidents of the period were useful and many issues of the *Arkansas Gazette* illuminating. All of the *Official Proceedings* of the Republican national conventions were important documentary sources. There are many good secondary sources on Republican party history. The most useful for the earlier period was Francis Curtis, *The Republican Party: A History of Its Fifty Years' Existence and a Record of Its Measures and Leaders, 1854-1904* (New York: G. P. Putnam's Sons, 1904), volume II. For the later period see Marion G. Merrill, *The Republican Command, 1897-1913* (Lexington, KY: UP of Kentucky, 1971). One chapter in Richard L. Niswonger, "Arkansas Democratic Politics, 1896-1920," unpublished Ph.D. dissertation, U. of Texas, 1973, was helpful as was his "Arkansas and the Election of 1896," *Arkansas Historical Quarterly*, XXXIV (1975). For the race issue and the Arkansas Republican party see Hanes Walton, Jr., *Black Republicans: The Politics of the Black and Tans* (Metuchen, NJ: Scarecrow, 1975); Tom Dillard, "To the Back of the Elephant: Racial Conflict in the Arkansas Republican Party," *Arkansas Historical Quarterly*, XXXIII (1974); and Willard B. Gatewood, Jr., "Arkansas Negroes in the 1890's: Documents," and "Negro Legislators in Arkansas, 1891: A Document," both in the *Arkansas Historical Quarterly*, XXXIII (1974) and XXXI (1972). For the agrarian coalition with Arkansas Republicans see Clifton Paisley, "The Political Wheelers and the Arkansas Election of 1888," *Arkansas Historical Quarterly*, XXV (1966). Two excellent dissertations covering this period were Joe T. Segraves, "Arkansas Politics, 1874-1918," University of Kentucky, 1974, and Garland E. Bayliss, "Public Affairs in Arkansas, 1874-1896," University of Texas, 1972.

Chapter Six: *Diplomatic Career*. The only extensive work done on this phase of Clayton's life was William H. Burnside, "Powell Clayton: Politician and Diplomat, 1897-1905," unpublished Ph.D. dissertation, University of Arkansas, 1978, based on United States Department of State, *Despatches from United States Ministers to Mexico, 1823-1906*, Record Group 59, M97; *Diplomatic Instructions of the Department of State, 1801-1906: Mexico*, Record Group 59, M77; and *Notes to Foreign Legations in the United States from the Department of State, 1834-1906: Mexico*, Record Group 59, M99. The most significant secondary sources were William I. Buchanan, "Latin America and the Mexican Conference,"*The Annals of the American Academy of Political and Social Science*, XXIII (1903); John W. Foster, "The Pan American Conferences and Their Significance," *Annals* XXVII (1906); Robert Gregg, *The Influence of Border Troubles on Relations between the United States and Mexico, 1876-1910* (Baltimore: Johns Hopkins, 1937); Norris Hundley, *Dividing the Waters: A Century of Controversy Between the United States and Mexico* (Berkeley: U of California P, 1966); Francis J. Weber, "The Pious Fund of the Californias," *Hispanic American Historical Review*, XLIII (1963); and A. Curtis Wilgus, "The Second International American Conference at Mexico City," *Hispanic American Historical Review*, XI (1931).

Chapter Seven: *Family Life*. The most important source of information for this chapter were letters from and conversations with Mrs. Diane Medlicott, great-granddaughter of Powell Clayton. Diane is the daughter of Kathleen Montpellier, Clayton's oldest granddaughter. Mr. Ronald Medlicott has also been very helpful. He has been in the family for many years as the husband of Clayton's youngest granddaughter, Marie, who was killed in a department store fire in 1967. In 1976 Ronald Medlicott married Diane Montpellier. Together with Clayton's great-great-grandson, Vincent Goffinet, they have supplied the author with traditional family history and with many letters written by Clayton, his children, and grandchildren. Other family information came from Thomas Jefferson Clayton, *Rambles and Reflections* (Chester, PA, 1892) and from Powell Clayton's great-nephew's unpublished manuscript, John W. LeBosquet, "William Henry Harrison Clayton: A Biographical Sketch" (Wichita, KS, n.d.). *The Encyclopedia of the New West* (Marshall, TX: United States Biographical Publishing, 1881); Peggy Jacoway, *First Ladies of Arkansas* (Kingsport, TN: Southern Publishers, 1941); and an article by Bernice Cole in the 6 April 1979 *Arkansas Gazette* gave additional insights. See also Anne McMath, "Adeline McGraw Clayton," *First Ladies of Arkansas:Women of Their Times*. (Little Rock: August House, 1989).